Very truly

Your obt Servant

David Barker

POEMS

BY

DAVID BARKER,

WITH

Historical Sketch

—BY—

HON. JOHN E. GODFREY.

BANGOR:
PRESS OF SAMUEL S. SMITH & SON.
1876.

PREFACE.

On the 7th of July, 1874, my brother David wrote me an affectionate letter, concluding as follows:

"I shall do my best to live here below a while longer, but the chances look doubtful. Should we not meet again, do what you think best with the songs I have sung here, and I promise you one from beyond at the earliest possible hour, and from a harp attuned by your angel daughter Evvie, if I can find her upon the same plane upon which I am permitted to enter, with the lingering earth stains which may be found upon me."

In a few weeks afterward he was at my office in Bangor, tottering upon his cane, and there for the first time met Mr. Wiggin, the author of the "Epistle to Davie," appended to the biographical sketch, by Judge Godfrey, herein published. It gave me great pleasure to introduce the poets to each other. At the close of the interview, David said to Mr. Wiggin: "I don't know whether the world will remember me, Ed., but if they do, you shall live with me;" and turning to me, said: "See to it, Lew., that we go down through the years together."

After his death, in September following, his widow sent me all his manuscripts, as left by him, carefully folded up, with the following direction pinned on them:

MEMORANDUM.—JULY 15, '74.

The accompanying manuscript contains all the poems I have preserved, and from which the proper selections are to be made, if published. I regret that some scraps contained herein were written, and that I have not health to copy the good and reject the other. If my brother Lewis survives me, and publishes my poems, he will see to it.

D. B.

Though shrinking from the thought of inviting public attention to myself, and all unfitted for this kind of work, I dared not decline the thrice imposed duty thus enjoined upon me by one so dear to me.

The following volume contains by far the greater part of what he has written. I have carefully preserved and had bound, in two volumes, every scrap of his original manuscript, that somebody may correct any error I may have committed, in my selections or rejections, if it shall ever be deemed worth the while to do so.

The "First Courtship" has never before been published. Almost every other production in this volume has, within the last twenty-five years, been seen floating upon the sea or in the eddies of American newspaperdom. "Early Recollections" was his first and "Katahdin Iron Works" was his last publication. In my selections I have been governed by the single rule of excluding every word which I thought he might now regret having written.

LEWIS BARKER.

Bangor, January, 1876.

CONTENTS.

MORAL AND SENTIMENTAL.

PATRIOTIC.

MISCELLANEOUS.

BIOGRAPHY.

Nearly twenty years ago there appeared in the New York *Evening Post* the following stanzas:—

MY CHILD'S ORIGIN.

One night, as old Saint Peter slept,
He left the door of Heaven ajar,
When through, a little angel crept,
And came down with a falling star.

One summer, as the blessed beams
Of morn approached, my blushing bride
Awakened from some pleasing dreams,
And found that angel by her side.

God grant but this—I ask no more—
That when he leaves this world of sin,
He'll wing his way for that blest shore,
And find the door of Heaven again.

The lines immediately attracted attention and were copied extensively into the newspaper press throughout the country. Governor Andrew was so impressed by them that he carried them with him, affirming that they were "the sweetest lines he ever read."

Of course their paternity was soon discovered, and the name of David Barker became familiar. That such charming verses should escape the profane hand of the parodist was too much to expect, when those of Longfellow and Whittier could not. They came out from under it, however, with a greater lustre, and, notwithstanding the momentary shock to his sensibilities when it first fell under his eye, Mr. Barker had the satisfaction which Mrs. Sarah J. Hale experiences in regard to an early poem of her own, which had been subjected to many travesties, that it "has done a world of good, nevertheless;" and of knowing that his little gem would sparkle when parody and parodist were buried in oblivion.

Other productions of Mr. Barker have added no little to his reputation. Among them "The Old Ship of State," "The Under Dog in the Fight," "The Covered Bridge," and "The Empty Sleeve," have met with great favor. That, however, which in the opinion of many of his friends, will be most enduring, is his longest poem, "My First Courtship." There is so much apparent reality in the scenes described in that poem, and many of the forms of expression adopted are so happily introduced, that the people of his region, to whom their significance is clear, will recur to it with delight.

In the last years of his life, this poem was read by Mr. Barker to many audiences in different parts of the State, and from the admirable faculty he had of inoffensively pressing into his service, on occasion, the names of prominent individuals in the assembly, as if they were of the *dramatis personæ*, he created great amusement among his hearers.

Mr. Barker was born and reared, and spent the chief part of his life, in the thrifty agricultural town of Exeter, in the State of Maine. At the time of his birth, the population of that town, not five hundred, was composed chiefly of sensible, hard-working, enterprising people, who had immigrated thither poor, but with a determination to have a share in the world's prosperity. Among these pioneers was Nathaniel Barker, a native of Exeter, New Hampshire, then late a resident of Limerick, Maine. He came in 1802, and was instrumental in having the name of his native town given to this one of his adoption. He took up a farm, and, in 1807, married Sarah Pease, then of Exeter, but born in Parsonsfield, Me., a wife not behind him in heroism and enterprise. Ten children were the fruit of the marriage, the sixth of whom was David. Hon. Noah Barker was the oldest, and Hon. Lewis Barker was the seventh. Both of these gentlemen have held prominent positions in the State.

David was born September 9, 1816. When in his seventh year, the family were thrown into deep affliction by the death of the father, who was accidentally killed, in Bangor, by his team, in 1823. The suddenness of the calamity was sufficient to unnerve a person of less sensibility than the widow; but, though overwhelmed with grief, she at once comprehended, and bravely assumed, her double responsibility. It was important that she should know what were her resources for the support of her family. She found that her husband's estate must be administered upon, and relying mainly upon herself, she commenced early proceedings in the Probate Court, riding on horseback nearly thirty miles over devious bridle-paths and rough roads, to and from Bangor, in doing her business. She discovered that the estate was insolvent; and all she could obtain, with which to sustain her young family, was an allowance of three hundred dollars from the Judge of Probate, and a trifle of dower. But, with this little property and the encouragement of her older children, she resolved to make the attempt to live independently of outside assistance. She was upon the farm that her husband had purchased, but it was incumbered for more than it was worth. She and her children determined to redeem it, and they did; and now, at the age of eighty-six, she lives upon that farm.

Hon. Josiah Crosby, in his eloquent eulogy upon the subject of this sketch, notices the mother and family in the following language:—

"The mother was a woman of great energy of character, and strong religious faith. A family council was held at which it was resolved by the mother and concurred in by all those of the children of sufficient maturity of judgment to take part in the deliberations, not to separate, but to keep the family together, seeking no aid from relatives or strangers, but relying upon their own strength, and faith in God. The event has signally justified the wisdom of their resolve. The children all grew up, were well educated, and have all attained to and maintained a highly respectable position in society. In contributing to this happy result, the children have ever been justly proud to acknowledge their obligations to the influence of their mother's energy, wisdom and force of character. I have also ever believed that to the precepts of their elder brother Noah, but more especially to the quiet, unobtrusive but constant force of his example in integrity, industry and perseverance, much of their success in life is to be attributed. Their bereaved condition, instead of depressing their spirit, taught them habits of self-reliance, inspired energy, and fitted them to combat with the world perhaps with more success in after life, than if the great misfortune of their youth had not befallen them. The case may perhaps afford another illustration of the truth of the trite remark, that our greatest afflictions are often blessings in disguise."

David was too young at the time of his father's death to be of much assistance to his mother, but he early learned that he must depend upon himself when he had attained to sufficient age. He had ambition for knowledge, and was an apt scholar. Until about sixteen years of age, he had only the advantages of the common school. He had, then, by his industry, obtained sufficient means to enable him to attend the Academy in Foxcroft. In that excellent school he made such proficiency that, after a time, he was employed in it as an assistant. After leaving Foxcroft, he engaged in school teaching, and soon became so popular as a teacher that his services for common schools were always in demand. He was employed in his own and neighboring towns, and was at one time called away from home as far as Eastport, where he exercised his skill as instructor very satisfactorily.

But it was not his intention to make teaching his vocation. He thought that a trade would be more manly, as well as more profitable, than the profession of a pedagogue. And he was correct, for, in that day, the common school master was deemed a sort of necessary evil, and paid accordingly. He chose the trade of blacksmith. He was too frail, however, for the severe toil required by that occupation, and, after a short apprenticeship, his health broke down, and he left it to be always an invalid.

When Samuel Cony (the late Governor Cony,) first established himself as a lawyer in Exeter, Mr. Barker entered his office to qualify himself for the profession of the law. He made due proficiency, and was with that gentleman until he removed to Oldtown. He then went into an office in Bangor, and, not long afterwards, was admitted to the Bar. He opened his law office in Exeter, and was in successful practice there until within two or three years before his death, when his physical system had become so shattered that he did little else than occasionally occupy himself in poetical composition; reading sometimes in public when he felt strong enough. But the time came, at last, when he had to relinquish that delightful employment.

While on a visit to his friends in Bangor—yet maintaining the belief that many years were in store for him—he quietly sunk into his final slumber. He died at the house of his brother, Mark Barker, Esq., September 14, 1874, at the age of fifty-eight years.

At the next term of the Supreme Judicial Court, in October, Judge John A. Peters presiding, the following resolutions of the Penobscot Bar were presented by Hon. Josiah Crosby, accompanied by an eloquent and touching tribute to his memory.

Resolved, That the members of Penobscot Bar have heard with deep sensibility the announcement of the death of Brother David Barker, a member of this Bar.

That, as a mark of respect to his memory, we desire to put on record our cheerful testimony to his ability as a lawyer, his amiability, urbanity and unquestioned integrity; and we shall ever remember with much interest those other gifts by which he was distinguished in the lists of poetic fame.

That these proceedings be recorded, and a copy of the same be communicated to his family by the Secretary in token of our sympathy with them in their great bereavement.

Mr. Crosby, who knew him well—having for many years been his nearest neighbor of the profession—said:

"His ability and attainments in the legal profession, notwithstanding constant feebleness of health, were highly respectable; and there is no doubt that had his health been firm, and his physical powers equal to his mental, he might have attained to a distinguished position at the bar. Those of his brethren who some fifteen or twenty years since were accustomed to meet him in the conflicts of the arena, will well remember that victory over such an antagonist was not easily won. Feebleness of health, however, seated upon the nervous system had a tendency to create a disrelish for the combative part of legal practice, which he finally relinquished, and gladly sought a purer and higher enjoyment in the fascinating realms of poesy.

In his practice he was ever honest and honorable. His word was never doubted. Sympathy for the distressed, was a most prominent trait. He never oppressed the poor, never treated them with haughtiness, never trod upon their feelings. His heart and purse were ever open to the calls of charity. His poem on the Masonic sign of distress could never have originated with one not in sympathy with the unfortunate. It was this trait, undoubtedly, which, when many years ago to be called an abolitionist was in the minds of most people, to be called by a term of reproach; in the times when Wm. Lloyd Garrison was mobbed, and churches were burned, I say it was in great measure this trait which led him to break loose from all his political affiliations, and to claim for himself the appellation of the unpopular abolitionist. He was not only honest in his business relations, but he had in a marked degree that higher type of honesty, which caused him to be faithful in the expression of his convictions, and to follow them to their logical result.—He desired not the rewards of political ambition. The only political position he ever held was that of representative in the Legislature, which he filled one year at the request of his townsmen, with much credit.

No man was ever more free from the trammels of dogmas, creeds and traditions, but his religious faith was strong. He had a firm belief in an overruling Providence; the life hereafter; and that death was but an entrance to a higher state of existence; as that impressive poem, "The Covered Bridge," will readily bring to the mind. His religion, however, was not of the boisterous kind. It consisted in doing to others as he would have others do to him, rather than the observance of forms and ceremonies, and the utterances of emotion.

In one department, that of poetry, he had obtained a distinguished reputation, a lot which seldom happens to travelers in the rugged and difficult paths of the legal profession. Poetry he loved. The muses answered kindly to his call, and it was a source of just satisfaction to him, that he had written some things which would live after him. The "Sign of Distress," "The Covered Bridge," "The Empty Sleeve" and many others of his productions, and poems will not soon die."

Judge Peters bore testimony to his excellent qualities in the following graceful response:

"*Gentlemen of the Bar:*—I am happy that it falls to myself as a member of this Court, to express a cordial concurrence in the sentiments contained in your resolutions, and in the warm and glowing tribute of respect paid to the deceased by your committee, in presenting them.

I first knew the deceased, when I came to the Bar of this county, about thirty years ago. I very well remember his encouraging expressions to me when I was engaged in trying the first cause that I ever tried in this court. After I had gained some position at the bar, in the trial of causes, he often employed me for his clients. I do not now recollect that we were ever opposing attorneys, in any litigated case. We were often together. In our professional intercommunication, he wrote to me many letters—some of them in verse—of a humorous character, containing flashes of wit and fun. Our relations led me to know him well.

Although he was not lacking in any of the intellectual qualities which would have made him a successful advocate, still he was disinclined to take upon his shoulders the heavy responsibilities and burdens which an advocate has to bear. But he was a most valuable associate. His court business was always perfectly prepared. There was great method and completeness in his preparation of causes for trial. His perceptions were very quick and exact; and his whole soul was engaged in any cause undertaken by him.

After all, professional life, evidently, was not entirely in accord with his predominating tastes; and for that reason, he has established before the world more position and reputation out of, than in the courts.

He was extensively known and appreciated *as a man.* He was invariably courteous and cordial. It was always pleasant to meet him. His nature was kindly and sympathetic, and sensitive. This led him to be, sometimes, easily elated or depressed. Still he had great firmness of purpose and serious and settled convictions, although never obtruded upon anybody or offensively expressed. He had no toleration for the shows or shams of society, either in the social or the moral world. We all very well remember how well he loved his country during the late war; how absorbed he was in its exciting scenes; what an enthusiast he was about the questions, regarded by him as affecting human freedom! He found in those stirring events an inspiration for that peculiar literary effort for which he possessed a gift.

His poetical productions will be the principal monument to his fame and memory. I frequently urged him to collect and publish them, while he lived. I was satisfied that they would meet with marked public favor, which would have been a great gratification to him. But nothing would have more deepy affected him, in his life time, than an anticipation and belief—if such a thing could have been—that this grateful and tender tribute was in store for his memory from this bar. My personal sentiment and feeling is, that observances like this should not pass into neglect, or out of our esteem. They may serve to stimulate a motive for honorable conduct at the bar. There can be no better memorial offered for honorable professional life than a tribute from the fraternity, placed upon the records of the courts where honorable character has been attained in the practice of the law.

The name and character of our lamented brother will long be fresh within our memories. He will be long remembered by us for his cordial, personal greetings; his pleasant anecdotes, and playful remarks; his activities and sympathies in all the events that for many years passed about us; his gifts in poetical effusions that hit off our local habits, customs and character; his own good character as a man, and his unsullied reputation as a practitioner at this bar.

It was sad to see him in the prime of manhood pass away. His death has cast a gloom and shadow upon our path. It is another reminder that life is but "a vapor that appeareth for a little time, and soon vanisheth away."

But we have the consolation that death is the beginning of immortality. As Longfellow expresses it—

"There is no death!
What seems so is transition."

In compliance with your request the resolutions of the bar are ordered to be entered on the records of this Court; and as a further mark of respect this Court will now be adjourned."

Mr. Barker left a widow—the daughter of Timothy Chase, Esq., of Belfast—and a son and a daughter. While not what would be called "a money getter," yet he left a tolerable estate. When his unpromising start in life, and his struggles always with disease, from his maturity, are considered, there must be a feeling of satisfaction that his success was so great. As a poet he will live. There are many gems from his pen that cannot die. The touching references to his mother, in several of his poems, will endear him to all who maintain their regard for the filial sentiment, and they are legion.

His townsmen manifested their regard for his abilities by electing him a Representative to the Legislature of 1872. But, though he was a useful member, and very popular, yet this kind of public life was not to his taste, and he had no desire to be returned. His modesty led him to doubt his right to any peculiar public regard, and he was often subject to surprises. That his poetical fame should bring to him the degree of A. M., from Bowdoin College, was as gratifying as it was unexpected. From individuals in different parts of the country, who had been moved by one or another of his poems, he received letters expressing deep obligations for the pleasure he had afforded them. But the surprise which, of all others, most affected him, was a poetical greeting he received from one who had been a soldier in the war of the Rebellion, of whom he then had never heard, but whom he afterwards met and thanked for his charming compliment—assuring him that, should his own effusions be remembered, these verses should share their fortune, so far as he could make provision therefor. It is fitting that they should have a place here.

The stanzas were printed in the Bangor Daily Whig and Courier, from which they were taken, with the preliminary remarks of the editor, Capt. C. A. Boutelle.

EPISTLE TO DAVIE.

BY EDWARD WIGGIN, JR.

These lines were intended for perusal only by the "Bard of Exeter," Me., David Barker, Esq., to whom they were addressed; but having come into our possession, we have taken the liberty of giving them that wider publicity to which their exceptional merit entitles them.—EDITOR.

My Davie dear, I lang hae thought
  That I suld like to know ye,
If but to mak' acknowledgment
  O' a' the debt I owe ye;
A debt o' gratitude untold,
  For strains sae sweet an' true, mon,
They struck my heart's maist tender chords,
  An' thirled them thro' an' thro', mon.

I've aften thought, 'I'll write the lad,'
  But modesty restrained me,
(It's been the bane o' a' my life,
  An' muckle it has pained me);
An' something said "Why tak' the pains?
  Why, mon, gin ye had wrat it,
He'll tak no notice o't ava
  Ye'll never ken he gat it."

But this ae morn when a' alane,
  An' time was hinging heavy,
Said I (I've said't a thousand times),
  "By Jove! I'll write to Davie,"

If he'll disdain a brither mon
  Because *he's* ca'd a poet,
Then ilka line belies him sure,
  His verses dinna show it.

I mind ae night in days lang syne,
  When by the camp-fire seated,
A brither soldier, sin' gane hame,
  Some lines o' yours repeated.
'Twas that aboot the 'Empty Sleeve,'
  It moved us a' to tears,
Tho' some o' us had grown sae hard
  We hadna greet for years.

An' years agane, when my sweet bairn
  Went o'er my heart to heaven,
An' frae my vera saul the light
  O' life seemed darkly driven,
I chanced ae day in some auld prent
  Thae lines o' yours to meet,
Aboot the 'Shepherd an' the Lamb,'
  An' oh, they seemed sae sweet.'

O Davie, mon, 'tis sweeter far
  To speak a word o' cheer,
To some puir brither sinner's heart,
  When a' seems mirk an' drear;
To cast ae glintin' ray o' light
  Across some darkened way—
'Tis sweeter far than warld's applause,
  Or gear that can decay.

But gin I dinna hae a care
  I'll e'en get melancholie,
An' then my muse (she's weak at best)
  Will sure desert me wholly.
Not aye ye rhyme o' tender themes,
  But aften i' your daffin',
Ye rin us aff a random screed,
  Near pits us dead wi' laughin'.

Your 'Bevelled Grunstane' true to life—
  How aft I've seen sic misers,
Sae mean they aye o'erreach themsel's
  In spite o' a' advisers.
An' thae queer lines ye read the day
  The sodgers met thegither,
Aboot 'Auld Willey's gaun t' enlist—
  'Twas better e'en than tither.

Your 'Dog'——— but gin I name them a'
  'Twad mak' owre lang a letter,
But ilka ither ane ye write
  Is sure to be the better;
An' just the ither day ye met
  Wi' frien's frae far awa',
An' thrawed us aff the 'Bradbury Boys,'
  By Jove! 'ts the best o' a'.

There's ae thing aye aboot yure rhymes
  That draws me kin'ly to 'em,
An' that's the strain 'o manliness
  That's ever rinnin' thro' 'em;

Nae sickly, sentimental whine,
  Nor cynical compleenin',
But aye aff han', right honest words,
  That hae an honest meanin'.

Lang may ye live to court the muse,
  An' may she ne'er desert ye;
May sorrow ne'er yure ingle blight,
  An' poverty ne'er hurt ye;
An' hoping sune that you an' I
  May chance to meet thegither,
I sign mysel' for weal or woe,
  Yure loving frien' an' brither.

FORT KENT, MAINE.

MY FIRST COURTSHIP.

MY FIRST COURTSHIP.

Who seeks to drown the heart's first love
  Will find it harder, even,
Than that old task, in Palestine,
  To stone the truth from Stephen.

For dross, which I may never need,
  With songs, which none should sing or write,
Through lunacy I have agreed
  To come and make you laugh to-night.

The bond is signed, and stamped and sealed,
  And I must execute the job,
Though every smile that you may yield
  Has cost my bleeding heart a throb.

For, ah, my mortal brothers,
 The misery that thrives in me
 They take to some distillery,
And make it joy for others.

I come here with the tongue of rhyme,
 To tell you for your pelf,
What each of you may know and feel,
 But cannot tell yourself.

I come to make your hearts elate,
 And drain your eyes of tears,
And all beneath the sagging weight
 Of more than fifty years.

But then, my friends, I deem it meet
 To tell you plain, to make you laugh,
I've now and then a grain of wheat
 Mixed with a mighty lot of chaff.

My reason for the scrimp is this:—
 Some stomachs hold a frightful heap,
And 'twill not pay to fill them up,
 Unless the food comes mighty cheap.

Besides, whene'er I read my rhymes,
  And keenly look my audience o'er,
I always see (or find at times)
  Among my crowd one fool or more.

The conscientious, brainless man
  Puts out his scrip for real chaff,
And 'twere gross fraud upon the fool
  Should I not try to make him laugh.

But as the thing looks here to-night,
  (I state the fact 'twixt you and me)
If laughing is confined to fools,
  Then fools have the majority.

I like the blessed law of change,
  And so, to-night, I change my rules,
And every one who will not laugh,
  I enter on my list of fools.

Each mortal has a two-fold form,
  Distinct as saint and sinner,—
One is the outer form, you see,
  The other is the inner.

I shall speak words to many a soul,
  Who, coming out to hear me,
Would like to use, at many a point,
  His outer form to cheer me.

It may not do—convention's codes
  Stand grimly to deride one,
So cheer me with your *inner* form,
  If not with the outside one.

Through all the pestering scenes of life
  Each brother has his special need,
Some need religion—some a wife—
  A dog, or a velocipede—
And many on this earthly ball,
To keep them straight should have them all,

My Muse knows no partiality—
  But sends her notes, so thrilling,
For satin, broadcloth, and for silk,
  And also for blue drilling.

I have seen flirting oft afar
In Tuilleries and Boulevard;

I have seen courting going on
  Up in the Scottish highlands,
In Celtic hut, and Switzer's cot,
  And in the sea-girt islands;

But know not what true love may be,
  When dosed and dabbled out among
  The numerous wives of Brigham Young,
Or peddled out to two or three.

I cannot talk to you in words
  Which you can fully understand,
Who, born with gold spoons 'tween the lips,
  Or some proud scepter in the hand,
And never felt Fate's grabs and grips;
But you, who born, as I was born,
  In modern or in earlier times,
With sand and hay-seed in your hair,
And grew, like Topsy, without care—
  I sing to *you* in these odd rhymes.

When, for the first time in your life,
You dream of those strange words, *a wife*,
And from your mother's cupboard go,
And the first time in earnest throw,

In kind of bashful, leisure haste,
Your green arm 'round a green girl's waist,
If, like the mariner, when tossed
On wave, with chart and compass lost,
Who trusts his helm, when tempest driven,
To the old dipper star in heaven;
She, in her new and girlish bliss,
Will trust your first raw, country kiss,
Then look as happy 's though she knew
She'd got one hard week's washing through,—
And if it gives your nerves a twist,
And sends a prickling through the wrist,
Much like a tunk upon the point
Or apex of your elbow joint,
Brings from your stomach long-drawn sighs,
And pumps up water through the eyes,—
Then bet that you are both in love,
And that the match was made above;
That you and she, through smiles and tears,
Will live and love through life's long years,—
She turning with her wealth of soul,
As turns the needle to the pole;
Then clinging through your rise and fall,
As clings the ivy to the wall,—
Unless some fancy, curl-haired fop

Wades in, and breaks love's crockery up.
That thing was done, as you shall see,
Betwixt Almira Grant and me.

Yes, I have loved like other folks,
  Who've been to institutions,
Though love, like whiskey, different works
  On different constitutions.

A man may blindly love for years,
  Without his neighbors knowing it,
As one may own the rarest gem,
  And not be always showing it.

'Twas at a country paring-bee
  I met the fair Almira,—
I reckon from that blessed day
  As Arabs from Hegira.

I waited on her home that night,
  And spent the coming day with her,
And fixed my mouth a thousand times
  To ask if I might stay with her.

Upon my chair I played old reels,
  By drumming with my fingers,

And felt, no doubt, as darkness feels
  Which round the daylight lingers.

We both were verdant as the blade
  Of grass in summer weather;
But then methought that we were made
  To ripen off together.

Some bards would make her free from sin,
  And say that angels chased her,
To feast their eyes upon her skin,
  Which shamed pure alabaster,—

And paint her graceful, swan-like neck—
  Her flowing auburn tresses—
Her Chinese feet, and arching back—
  Her Aidenn-born caresses:

Her laughing eyes and sunny cheek,
  Her breath so pure and balmy,
Her pearly teeth, erect and trained,
  Like soldiers for the army.

In building roads or telling yarns
  I'm death against this crooking,—

I only say that she was more
  Than decently good looking.

She claimed no blood from royal fools—
  Her father was a yeoman,
Who owned his farm and farming tools,—
  Her mother was a woman.

One thing can truthfully be said,
Almira would not crawl from bed,
  And sit two hours a yawning;
She seldom slopped and never sloshed,
Her back hair combed and face she washed,
And then the darling girl, beside,
Would always have her shoe-strings tied
  The first thing in the morning.

Whene'er she stood, Almira looked
  Straight as a gun from end to end;
She was not twisted, warped nor crook'd,
  By what they call the Grecian bend.
My neighbor's girl—Placenta Ladd—
That Grecian bend, she had it bad,
She caught it down at Saratogue,
From one who had a foreign brogue.

In gazing on some lovely form,
Right from the hand of Nature warm,
Although your love be sizzling hot,
The fear of fist or pistol shot
From lover, father, or from brother,
Or swinging broomstick from the mother,
  May silence you from winking
Too often at the luscious dear,
But, thank the Lord, one thing is clear:—
Our courts have not decided yet
A lovesick fellow cannot sit
  Stock still and keep a thinking.

In those old times if we should court
  Two girls of Jones' or Hilliard's,
Who weighed one hundred sixty pounds,
  Each, by her father's steelyards.

One thing is sure as time and tide,
  That we were safe in betting,
'T was solid girl, and nothing else,
  That you and I were getting.

But now the flame you're "fluking" with
  Perhaps is mostly "boughten,"

Made up in part of rubber goods,
  And part of cork and cotton.

Those peeping mole hills 'neath her chin,
  To craze some frail beholder,
Perhaps are gutta percha balls
  A peddling Jew has sold her.

And ten to one, the bridal night
  May prove your festive charmer
Has nought but artificial legs—
  Those patent legs by Palmer.

And she, whom paste has made as fair
  As Whittier's Maud Muller,
May prove by touch of Castile soap
  Quite of a different color.

The girls we picked in days of yore,
  Before we had to choose 'em,
We peaked to notice if they wore
  Crash towels in the bosom.

I care not what another says—
As woman rigs up now-a-days,

It muddles up your head
To know which part to call your wife—
The real partner of your life—
The part that she takes off at night,
By gas, or lamp, or candle light,
Or the part that goes to bed.

What shall be done, cries every one,
From priest to the wood-sawyer,—
I give advice, not as a saint,
But give it as a lawyer:—

Have faith that all is genuine;
But ere the anxious lover
Invests his all in fancy stocks,
He'd better look them over.

Some things the old folks seemed to prize
Above her being fair:
Her mother told me that her girl
Was rugged as a bear.

And then the old man bragged, that she
Was built just like her mother;

Was just as limber as an eel,
And just as tough as leather.

He bragged, that she was hard as horn,
And she could stand the hardest knocks,
And never yet had lost a meal
But once, when she and Huldah Neil
Took cold one night in husking corn—
That Fall, they had the chicken-pox.

When racked by pain and bowed by care,
Like most of us at present,
I think each stricken heart should feel
That "tough and rugged as a bear,"
And "just as limber as an eel,"
Are phrases rather pleasant.

A healthy soul we all should prize,
But then 'tis doubtful whether
You well can run a rugged soul
And feeble form together.

If soul or body gets the pole,
Each makes bad time forever,
The same as Bonner's horse of fame—

I think that Dexter is his name—
The same perchance, or even worse,
If geared, when trotting on the course,
  Beside a yearling heifer.

Our chance for courting was not big,
  I and my fair Almira;
Upon that night I reckon from
  As Arabs from Hegira.

One side the room the old folks slept—
  Her father and her mother—
The swifts, wheel, loom, and warping-bars
  Were standing in the other.

The tom-cat and a cosset lamb
  Were in one corner lying,
While o'er our heads the pumpkin hung,
  My darling had been drying.

Above the belching back-logs, lain,
  The pig's and turkey victual
Was sweating on the iron crane,
  Within a five-pail kettle.

The cross-cut saw which never run,
  Except through stolen timber,
Stood grinning with its blunted teeth,
  Until its back grew limber.

The linen wheel, which whirred and sung
  By light from pitch-knots kindle,
Thrust out its homespun flaxen tongue
  From distaff to the spindle.

The sweeting-keg lay on the floor,
  The "lobbing" dish lay by it;—
Those things they used when callers came,
  To keep their young ones quiet.

Mid all inventions since those years,
  Oh deem it not surprising,
That we must use some sweetning kegs
  To keep our folks from rising.

A rundlet, filled with Shubael's rum,
  Which made him oft a noodle,
Was horsed beside his tenor drum,
On which, when Elder Hatch was there,
He played some old John Bunyan air;

But when the Elder whirled his gig,
And Shubael took an extra swig,
He dropped those airs from spirit lands,
And with his little horn-beam hands,
First pitched into the Chorus Jig,
  Then closed on Yankee Doodle!

Three boys were in a trundle-bed—
  One kicking with the colic;
Three girls, down through the knot-hole floor,
  Were peeping—full of frolic.

The old dog, with his glaring eyes,
  Lay on the hearth-stone near us,
As if to watch my girl and me,
  Like the fabled dog, Cerberus.

Their library, on the mantel-piece,
  Was of a rare selection—
They had all of the standard works,
  And but one work of fiction:

The Bible, Bunyan, Watts' Hymns,
  Which taught both me and you so—
The reader, speller, grammar-book,
  Arithmetic and Crusoe.

Grant said he always lived by plan,
For, on one shelf appointed,
There smoked the sulphur in the pan,
From which the children ointed.

One picture, on the moss-chinked wall,
She had of Susan Tainter,
Would knock old Michael Angelo,
Or any modern painter.

It looked some like a frightened bull
Hitched to a porter wagon;
She said that Susan painted it
For Michael and the Dragon!

The old flint gun—I see it still—
That queen's-arm used at Bunker's hill
By her great-grandsir Lowder,
Lay calmly in the hooks at rest,
But kept within its iron breast
One charge of shot and powder.

Those days I never would forget,
Till death my heart-strings sever;

Your modern style of etiquette
 Was then in fashion, never.

If mothers wished you not to stop
 To court a blushing daughter,
'Twas one blow with the handle mop,
 Or else some boiling water!

Ye need na piles of worldly gear,
Nor large amount of college lear,
By kintra wit and judgment clear,
 'Twill quick be found
If the auld mither of the dear
 Don't want ye round.

In writing rhymes, oh, what a band
Aft throng me frae the ither land,
And a' in circling hurdles stand,
 Though aft unseen—
That was Rob Burns' spirit hand
 On my machine.

Her mother, ere she went to bed—
 God bless the dear, old homespun saint—
The round pine kitchen table spread

With honey reeking from the bees,
With nut-cakes and some pigs'-foot cheese,
  In case the girl or I was faint.
I see that table standing there—
With top turned up it made a chair—
To give us one warm luncheon then,
(A theme fit for a seraph's pen)
Brought baked beans from the earthen pot,
An Indian loaf all piping hot—
  Whose worth the world has proven;
Whose inspirations oft I feel—
All reddening for the morning meal—
  Inside the old mud oven.

Then from the scripturés read a psalm,
  And prayed to Israel's God above,
To keep their darling girl from harm,
  And shield her in his arms of love.

Oh, had that mother's prayer been heard,
  No fitful touch from memory's breeze
Some string upon my harp had stirred,
  To bellow out such strains as these.

I, as the son-in-law of Grant,
  Had never caught the crazy whim,

To spend my hours in idle rant,
  And write these coming lines on him.

It may seem wrong—this bundling up—
This mixing in the self-same cup
  Life's awful facts with fiction;
It makes a mixture and a twist,
Like playing one short game of whist
  'Tween prayer and benediction.
But then, what can a fellow do
When love has loosened many a screw,
And warped and wrenched, as may be seen,
The gearing of his song-machine?
I'll do but this—to gain your pelf,
I'll let the old gear run itself.

LINES ON SHUBAEL, THE FATHER OF MY INTENDED.

Old Shubael Grant then bragged an hour
  Of every thing on earth he knew,
  And all he ever dreamed of, too,
How he had licked big Abel Tower,
  And knocked an eye and wisdom tooth
  Square down the throat of Orlan Booth;
How on one leg he used to stand,
  And box an hour with Rufus Carn;
And with an axe and flask in hand,

Had run the ridge-pole of a barn;
And how he always liked the fun
Of knocking hats with long-leg Banks,
And how they danced from sun to sun
At the last muster on the planks;
How, after dark, his old blind horse,
With heaves and lame in every foot,
He linked on old Jehial Morse,
And got a shoat and drink to boot;
How, when they raised the Libby mill,
He "rasseled" twice with Albert Hill,
And what a "most Jehovah flip"
He got from Albert's swinging trip;
But then for business, not for fun,
He tried the old half-buttock on—
When quick from science, not from strength,
He stretched old Albert twice his length;
How once a number twelve he wore—
Although his feet were small as mine—
To make them think 'twas neighbor Moore
Who plundered cedar o'er the line.
With iron heels and brads before,
The tracks resembled neighbor Moore.
And how he marketed his hay,
Not when the skies were bright and warm,

But always on a lowery day,
  And often through a driving storm,—
That half a ton, less tare and tret,
Was just twelve hundred when 'twas wet;
And what a joke he played on Howes—
  You know that Howes, that old blind Lem—
He milked two teats of both his cows,
  One season when he pastured them;
How good the Lord had been to him,
  For he had always had, through life,
A blessed rousing appetite,
  A rugged and a praying wife—
A wife who never had been slim—
  No "rheumatiz" or dizzy spell.
Their victuals always sat so well
  That they could eat, by day or night,
  Most any thing that they could bite;
And how he wiggled Ephraim Kidd,
  By making talk as fine as silk.
For, many a year ago, somehow,
He learned one lesson from his cow—
She always kept her garget hid,
  Until she showed it in her milk.
Though 'gainst the rules of fighting rings,
  He said he always felt

'Twas well, sometimes, to vary things,
  And strike below the belt;
And how, at Glover's nine-pin hall,
  He found one day in bowling,
There was as much in keeping slate himself,
  Or more, than there was in rolling.

How in the play, whate'er the name,
  One sacred rule he makes,
To end disputes about the game
  He always grabs the stakes.

Though he had strongest Bible faith,
  One thing he shouldn't try on—
He ne'er should try that Bible game
  To camp down with the lion;

For somehow he had always felt,
  Before they got through kissing,
Or got through with the play of lamb,
  The lamb would come up missing.

And how he always took his swigs
  In the old brown-earthen cup;
For one, he always meant to stick
  Right square to his bringing up;

And how it made him "cussed riled"
  To have it hinged by others,
Although his name was Shubael Grant,
  His father's name was Leathers;

And how at Pullen's piling bee
He whacked and whelted Simon Spear,
And warmed the wax within his ear—
  Yes, browsed him like a Saxon,
For speaking disrespectfully
  Of God and Andrew Jackson.

Then sipped—then told his girl and me,
How many a year ago, that he
Once stayed one night with Huldah Murch,
The very day she joined the church
  And worked for Captain Brown,
And how she had the smoothest skin
  Of any girl in town.

And how there was no woman born,
  Not e'en the wife of Elder Ayer,
Could hold a candle-stick to his
  In exhortation or in prayer.

How many a kicking colt he'd broke;
How many a pair and many a yoke
  Of kicking, hooking, sulky steers;
Then took some worm-wood for his cough,
Then pulled his shoes and stockings off,
  And cut his toe nails with the shears;
Then told me that he always waked
  From any little noise or sound,
But wanted me to feel at home—
  But hoped I wouldn't "larrup 'round."
Then put on airs and most polite,
He bade the girl and me good night.

Grant could not talk a word of Greek,
  And yet, from what I've heard them say,
  He'd steal more hoop-poles in a day
  Than Reverend Doctor Carlos Bond,
  Or learn'd Professor Enoch Pond
Could steal in cutting all the week.
Before we close earth's doubtful strife,
Or end this splendid fuss of life—
When fame and wealth and health have fled,
And friends to lean upon are dead—
Yes, when we're growing old and poor,
And hear the wolf around our door,—

But hoop-poles in the market sell,
It may be well, plain truth to speak,
If honestly, it may be well
To mix some hoop-poles with our Greek.

But after all, 'twixt you and me,
'Tis hard to tell you which is
The toughest load for mortals here—
The pinching load of poverty,
Or galling load of riches.

For I have ever dreamed this dream:
A hand, veiled out from human sight,
To meet our false weights on the beam,
Will fix the passive scales aright.

And each will find, throughout the strife—
Though fed from lean or fat ox—
Upon this battle-field of life,
Bull Run and Appomattox.

Have you ever yet felt as once I have felt,
What a world's wealth and glory are worth?
With an earthquake beneath, when around me they knelt,
With my faith, that was clear in my youth, blotted out

By a touch from the hand of the demon of Doubt,
When from pale mortal lips there ascended the cry
To a Power, dwelling up, as they said, in the sky;
When the summits were ripped from the mountains afar,
With the flames shooting out from their seams, like a star,
And strange mutterings came from the upheaving dell,
Like the rumblings that come from the bowels of hell,
And when, full on the ear, fell the sickening sound,
And we felt, as we hugged, like a child, to the ground,
  The uplift and the swing of the earth?
Since then I have dreamed, though I cannot tell why,
Of a Power in the spheres that is greater than I.

The fruits that grow from deeds of ill,
  Somehow, have ever brought to mind
That old and crazy cog-wheel mill,
  Where old John Buzzell used to grind.

Each for his grist must take his turn—
  Each form that shields a deathless soul—
And one tough lesson he must learn:
That though he curse, or though he pray,
While Justice grinds he takes his pay,
  To the last kernel of the toll.

Grant was an awful Democrat—
  To prove his hate of Whigs, 'tis said
He voted for Old Jackson once,
  Long after that old saint was dead.

He was a rigid Baptist, too;
  One day he cursed old Elder Pease,
The leader of the bolting crew,
  For preaching 'gainst Divine decrees.

The Baptists held their meetings there,
  And Shubael's only charge for rents
Was just the swigs he stole at prayer,
  From wines they brought for sacraments.

Grant was an office-seeker—some—
  He spared no pains—and spared no plan—
One year he paid a pint of rum
  To be elected tythingman:

He stood against Elkanah Brown—
  And, though the office didn't pay,
He swore he'd stop their strolling 'round
  Upon the holy Sabbath day.

And then he struck for power and place;
  Ah! how his cousins rent the air
The time he run with Uncle Mace,
  And beat him as highway surveyor.

This second office paid him best;
  He worked the taxes in his bills
Upon a fell-piece that he cleared:—
You knew that "cut-down" little west,
  And little east of Henry Hill's.

Sometimes I fear that, now-a-days,
  Our men of place have found the tracks
Into the cut-down where old Grant
  Worked out his neighbors' highway tax.

Old Shubael said he always prized
  The privilege of being found
  Upon the blessed, holy ground
Where converts went to be baptized.

Old Shubael was, one out of ten,
One of your handy kind of men—
For Shubael often stood or sat,
And held the convert's coat and hat;

Grant said that he could always tell
When pious folks were feeling well—
Then was a bully time, he said,
To show his spavined quadruped.
He said, in talking up a horse,
  No matter if he swapped or sold him,
The man of prayer and strongest faith
  Was apt to suck down what he told him.

Some traits I liked of Shubael Grant's,
  He played well on his drum and fife,
And, though he wore blue drilling pants,
  Was true and clever to his wife.

And, though he had a rattle head,
  At things Divine he wouldn't scoff,
And, though he went half choked, 'tis said,
  He never took his well-crank off.

He never changed nor flopped about,
  And now, wherever Grant may be,
In any world I have no doubt,
  He writes God with a little g;

And thinks as he did here in Maine,—
  He goes against each liquor law;—

He has no "nigger on the brain,"
  And always takes his whiskey raw.

If in the roaring pit, beneath,
  He'll fight, in lava to the knees,
Each sulphurous imp, who dares to breathe
  One word against Divine decrees!

That blessed wheat, mixed in with tares,
The pious mother's humble prayers,
  And love you harbor for her daughter,
You know will often make you stand
More lies, and brags, and drunks, and cheats,
  From the old father than you ought to.
And so, through prayers and rum and all,
I toughed it out at Grant's that Fall.

When Grant retired, so nearly nude,
  I felt upon my cheek a tear—
A blessed tear of gratitude;
  It was not that the coast was clear,
But ah, I felt 'twas plain to see,
That Shubael Grant had faith in me.
He knew I was not shuling 'round,
  Like Rufus York, that long-haired curse,

Who came that way and mended clocks,
  And fooled and ruined Mary Burse.
Poor Mary, and her mother, too,
  One night to Crowell's meadow came—
Poor Widow Burse to drown her grief,
  And Mary Burse to drown her shame.
When Mary and the Widow Burse,
  You know, within that brook were found,
And the crazed people thundered in
  From half a dozen miles around;—
How some the folks would stand and cry,
  While gazing on their dripping locks,
And some pile curses mountain high
  Around the wretch who mended clocks;
I love to hear a people pray—
  Then love to hear that people curse,
If they will swear, as on that day,
  While standing 'round poor Mary Burse.
But these my heart cannot approve,
  Whose pulses throb but one desire—
Whose eyes with measured winks will move,
And have the same look when they love—
  As when a building is on fire.

But what has this poetic rant
To do with courting 'Mira Grant?

I said, that Shubael Grant believed—
And Shubael Grant was not deceived—
That I had come, from mother's, bound
  For good and not for evil.
For, in five minutes, Shubael Grant
Turned over once, and took a cant
Upon sleep's inclined plane, it seems,
Which sluiced him to the land of dreams,
  While snoring like the devil.
Then Shubael's rest seemed sweet and deep,
Much like some certain lawyer's sleep—
For, though the bed is scrimped or wide,
Some lawyers lie on either side.

There's nothing for the realms of rhyme
  In future can occur,
To make me feel as, on that time,
  I sidled up to her.

I told my feelings square, if brusk—
  My talk seemed to amaze her;
Her heart beat so it broke her busk,
  Carved with her father's razor.

But, after I'd explained awhile,
  And got her more enlightened,

She seemed to act like other girls,
  More natural and less frightened.

For then she tied me up a wreath
  From flowers she had been culling—
The hollyhock, and butter-cup,
  The sunflower, pink, and mullen.

And then she sat and told how mean
  Jane Whitcomb cooks and washes,
And how the ring-tailed, striped bugs
  Had eaten up their squashes.

How Peavey's cats had lapped their cream,
  For yesterday she caught 'em;
And how she drove the measles out,
  And when and where she got 'em.

This was long before Jane Peaslie
  Had that whooping cough;
Long before her uncle Cyrus
  Made that yoke and trough—
Or New England rum was slandered
  By the lips of Gough;
Long before I fought my battle,

'Mid Plebeian throngs;
Long before I caught this rattle
From John Whittier's songs:
"Ho, fishermen, of Marblehead,
Ho, Lynn cordwainers, leave your leather,
And wear the yoke in kindness made,
And clank your needful chains together."

Now let me stop and say one verse,
I think is rather rich and mellow,
I've written better—written worse—
Though this was made by one Longfellow;
He wrote it at his old abode—
I understand he lives there still,
Near Guppy's, on the old cross road,
A nearer cut to Bunker's Hill:
"The heights by great men reached and kept,
Were not attained by sudden flight,
But they, while their companions slept,
Were toiling upward in the night."

In singing of the great man's climb,
Longfellow's words were plain and true;
The only doubt around his rhyme,
Is whether he meant me or you.

Now back to my Almira Grant:
  These tangent strides will prove my ruin;
I wander off and scoot and rant
  As Byron did in his Don Juan.
She told me how Lize Leathers walked,
  Or how she minced and wiggled,
And tried to tell me something else,
  But grabbed her nose and giggled.
How Rose Matilda Cole had got
  Red ears of corn at huskings;
How Grace Keziah Hodge had knit
  Jake Hasseltine some buskins.
Then, with a mild and reverent air,
  She told how Mary Eaton
Was just baptized, by Elder Pease,
  And how she spoke in meeting;

How all the converts in the town,
  "Brought out" at Deacon Horton's,
Would meet and tell experiences
  At the big barn of Norton's.
To build the towering church and spire,
  God's people, were not able,
And so, to hear their humble prayer,
The Lord would meet them anywhere—

In kitchen, grove, or stable.
With all the stains upon my soul,
Which years of sin have brought me,
I loathe the female tongue that scoffs
The faith my mother taught me:
A faith that tells to weary forms,
And hearts with sorrow riven,
Of healing balms in Gilead,
And better homes in heaven.
(These last two verses I have made,
So pious in expression,
Came from the heart, tho' they may seem
Unpardonable digression.)
You knew that frog-pond near our house,
On the old farm of mother's;
'Twas near the present grassy road
Which leads west from my brother's.
Some forty years ago, or so,
When there was fun in playing,
We boys would meet and spatter there,
Each evening after haying;
With little shirts and trowsers off,
We little human cattle,
Would splash around and duck our heads,
All eager for a battle.

I recollect (as plain as day)
One little Tommy Dyer,
Would always wade in to his knees,
But never wade in higher;
But I, your poet, feeling brave,
And finer than a fiddle,
Once waded in clear to my chin—
A foot above my middle.
But making then a slip or trip,
The fellows standing by me,
All had to join and fish me up,
Then pump me out and dry me,
So ever after that, when one
Would wish to wade in just for fun,
A piece of bed cord we had got
We tied around him, with a knot,
And held one end, when, in and in,
The fellow waded to his chin.
My love-sick brother, hear me through,
This sage advice I give to you:
When, with some female turtle-dove,
You come to the frog-pond of love,
Duck in and frolic as you please,
But then, like Tommy Dyer,
I wouldn't wade in to the knees;

But this strong resolution keep,
Wade in, perhaps, some ankle deep,
  But never wade in higher,
Until the bridal knot is tied
Within the bed-cord, 'round your side—
For ah! too late, it may be found,
  That fellow standing by you—
That cloven-footed fellow 'round—
May fish you up from off the ground,
  Then pump you out and dry you.

My Muse now takes another flop,
    This moment as she passes,
With one remark, and simply this:
When courting, filled with rustic bliss,
  We're often like the long-legged boy,
Who lived beneath the Hermon hill—
(I think his hat-band lives there still)
  Who, in his hour of awful joy,
Could not, for life, tell when to stop,
    The time he lobbed molasses;
When hogshead burst outside the door
Which led to big George Brackett's store,—
So, on one beauteous Summer day,
He lobbed and lobbed himself away.

Metempsychosis may be true:
  And in the future, dark and dim,
I may take on the poodle dog,
  Or e'en one of the seraphim.
If self must die, and change must come,
  How would my pulses thrill with joy,
To know that I could be transformed
  Into that long-legged Hermon boy.
Devoid of friction, care and pain,
  No aspiration, nor a throb,
Except to lie, while God should reign,
  Around some bursting cask and lob.

Now let me bounce back to that girl,
  So fair to each beholder,
And skip awhile what she told me,
  But tell you what I told her:

I told her how, that our steer calves,
  We swapped with Ivory Nutter,
Were having horns two inches long,
  And getting fat as butter;
How Chamberlain's sheep had owned her lamb—
  A fact which you and I know—
By putting Bose into the pen

Beside the young Merino;—
Not Chamberlain who, long moons ago,
Sent Paugus with a yell and bound—
That Lovell pond, or red skin foe,
Up to his upper hunting-ground;
Not he—one J. L. Chamberlain,
Who once was Governor of Maine,
Whose name may die in after times,
Unless I save him by these rhymes;
Whose name you all may soon forget,
Unless he asks a pardon yet.
He, with the loyal many,
For dealing out in that red fight,
With sword, and grape, and shot and shell,
On Little Round-Top, through that night,
That awful lurid dose of hell,
To those, by man and God accursed,
Turning the tide of treason first,
Way down in Pennsylvania.
But Chamberlain, whom you all well know,
Who lived nor'west of Alfred Rowe,
And sou'west of the Gilman hill,
And east of Eastman's cider mill—
His girl, you know, they called her Beck—
You know that mole upon her neck—

She wears the same knit garters still,
The bodice, with the skirt and frill,
The cotton-pads and raccoon fur,
When Abner Coburn courted her.
Beck gave Jim Blaine the mitten once,
Then took up with that perfect dunce,
That long nose Roswell Griffin,
Who came up from the Willard Bend
The day that our new barn was raised,
And drank new rum till nearly crazed,
Then won a gill from Moses Shead,
By standing longest on his head—
And lifted short-legg'd Deacon Beals
A dozen times, at the stiff heels—
Threw me at the backs and the arms'-end;
But then I tried a different lug,
And took him at the old side-hug,
And whopped and laid him on his mug,
In just a half a "jiffin."

This happy, short-legg'd Deacon Beals,
That Roswell lifted at stiff heels,
Was not the long-faced Deacon Beals
Who used to eat with us, and pray
An average of once a day;

And always lectured me on sin—
I see it now, but didn't then;
His prayers and appetite were good,
But then, to tell the honest facts,
Although my folks were mighty poor,
He never helped me cart manure,
Nor never helped me grind my axe,
Nor helped me chop a stick of wood.

In the last settlement above,
Whatever crimes or faults they prove,
Whatever else old Shubael lacks,
One thing his enemies will say,
He was a good man in his day
To break and swingle flax;
And, with two swigs of cherry rum,
Played nice tunes on his tenor drum,
And this was more, 'twixt me and you,
Than ever Deacon Beals could do.

Rebecca Chamberlain, ere she wed,
Had everything within her head;
For miles around, she knew them all,
By bonnet, overcoat, or shawl,
And I was told by Widow Moore,

That Miss Rebecca Chamberlain knew
The quantity and value, too,
  Of every rag of clothes you wore.
I think you knew poor Widow Moore?
  Though pure and holy, meek and mild,
Like a caged maniac, she swore,
  The night she lost her only child.
Sometimes a solace may be found
  To snatch and break the chastening rod,
And clank your galling chains, though bound,
  Square in the face and ear of God.

One day she told me, and she cried,
That winter that her husband died,
  She tended her own barn,
And spun with her poor widowed hands
  Five hundred skeins of yarn.
Ah! woman, in your gorgeous wealth.
  With false, perverted taste,
Who drizzle out a vapid life,
  Mid frippery and paste;
Come, I can teach you many a phrase,
  Yes, teach you how to speak,
Not only in my native tongue,
  But Latin, French, and Greek;

But cannot tell you what this means—
  She tended her own barn,
And spun with her poor widowed hands,
  Five hundred skeins of yarn.

I told of Lot Brown's piling-bee,
  The wrestle and the scuffle,
The French four and four-handed reel,
  The jig and double-shuffle;
And how we played "the needle's-eye
  Which carries its tape so true,
It has caught many a smiling lass,
  Now, lass, it has caught you."
I told her how, at Captain Ware's,
We fixed a quilt across two chairs,
Which Lydia Rich and Rachael Hart
Had stood, or fixed, two feet apart—
And how we got one Edward Fox—
'Twas not your learn'd Judge Edward Fox—
But he of the long and yellow locks,
He of the sunburnt, dog-tail curls—
To set him down between those girls,
When his true lover, quick, perhap,
Would come and sit upon his lap.
One fact was kept from Ed., you know:

The yawning, watery tub below.
Although we had a world of fun
With Edward Fox—the Baptist's son—
    That single hour's diversion
Sent Edward—son of Deacon Fox—
Half over with the orthodox.
  Although his heart and head were right—
Although, in soul, a Baptist still,
To gratify a stubborn will,
The lower half of Edward Fox
  Was ever, from that blessed night,
A rabid, blue-light orthodox,
    Or death against immersion.

I think 'twas after she had gone
And put another apron on,
And fixed, like other angel girls,
Those darling little water curls,
And hooked new nubs or ear-rings in,
Put on some other beads and pin,
Used camomile instead of musk,
And slipped in sly another busk,
And with her side-combs "primped," her hair
I told my dear Almira there—
Yes, spoke right out—that she was sweet,

And nearly good enough to eat;
She changed so quick from white to red,
It made a swimming in my head—
The doctors for a fee, you know,
Would call that swimming vertigo.
  Heaven only knows how we poor fools
Have toiled and sweat, from day to day,
To earn enough in part to pay
  For such old stuff they learn at schools.

As felt some Grecian mother's son,
  Who bore one of the classic names,
In boasting of a prize he won
  At those renowned Olympian games—
I strutted with a peacock's air,
And told my sweet Almira there,
How I and Dolly Peavey ran—
  And how I ran the faster;
When old York's Durham roared and pawed,
  As we went through the pasture.
I mind it well I tried to write
  Almira Grant a love-sick sonnet,
And how my heart would throb that night,
  As though it had a stone-bruise on it.

The darts of love I bravely met,
As Switzer Arnold Winkelried
Received the shafts within his breast,
When by the Austrian squadron pressed,
While leading through the Alpine fray
His comrades on that glorious day.
Young Love and I played hide and seek,
By skulking 'round, then darting in
The dimples on her rosy cheek
And creases of her double chin.

I told my dear Almira, there,
Who looked so fleshy and so fair,
(While sitting pretty near her chair)
How Rose Ross threw a ball of yarn
Into the well behind the barn;
Then wound it with a fellow—
How, one dark night, Robena Rand
Backed, with a looking-glass in hand,
Into Joe Hooker's cellar—
Not old fighting Joseph Hooker,
Who, above the clouds,
In the loom of the red angel,
Wove those dead men's shrouds;
Marching through those blistered regions,

With his blue and conquering legions,
  Bathing, as they trod,—
Bathing, from War's purple fountain,
The fevered brow of Look-Out Mountain,
  Half way up to God;—
And how we played old hide and seek;
  How Liz Jones tried to find me,
And how we used to "shave her down,"
By one song sung by Nancy Brown—
That blessed, sentimental song,
Which my scarred heart remembers long,
  "The girl I left behind me."
'Twas whistled, too, by Simon Phipps,
Whose lummox, loose, and lumbering lips,
We country boys, with wallets thin,
Had chartered for a violin.
Now Simon's notes were not so full
As those, perhaps, from Ole Bull,
And then, perchance, had not the ring,
Like that which fell from Mozart's string,
And not like Paganini's strains,
Which he would barter off for gains;
What Simon lacked in art sublime
He well made up in lips and time:
Sime learned his trade in Nature's shop,

And whistled until hired to stop.
Until my sun of life shall set,
These ancient legs can ne'er forget
Those gay old dances up at Drew's,
When girls flocked in with calf-skin shoes,
And never left the kitchen floor,
Till one good pair of taps they wore;
They never danced the eye to please—
They knew no polka or schottische;
They used no modern, mincing trips,
As though tight buckled 'round their hips;
Each had a dozen leathern straps,
When on the boards with us old chaps;
Our style was this—we "stronged" it through,
Led on by my friend, Hiram Drew;—
You know old Hiram Drew, of course,
The man who raised that trotting horse;
  Like the mad waves we surged about,
Through the blind whirl of jig and reel,
With flourish of the toe and heel—
  Until one side was "tuckered" out;
But taking breath and drying sweat,
We formed on for another set.

That ancient music from the lips
Of our hired whistler, Simon Phipps,
Was somewhat different, I should say,
From that I heard but yesterday,
In Reverend Wooster Parker's church,
(You see my Muse has taken a lurch)
There, one of the smooth haired fellows,
I noticed that he looked so grand—
Held that big lever in his hand,
And blew that organ bellows,
Beside that girl who oft was seen
To thump the keys on that machine,
When tunes slid out so smooth and still,
As grain slides from a winnowing mill.

And then I bragged how Bose would fight,
When Hi. Drew's dog would mad him,
And how, like blazes, Bright would pull
When Leather French would brad him.
Old Leather French, whose hermit name
From leathern garb was fitly given;
Whose fervent prayer, like incense came,
Upon each wandering breeze of heaven—
Who gave earth's favored lodgers room,
By sleeping in a pauper's tomb.

All unlettered, unknown, unattended and poor,
Both afoot and alone he went down to a shore,
With no weight at his heart, and no chafe, I am told,
With no chafe from the lugging of silver and gold;
With a gaze at a mount, in a summer-like land;
With a seat by a form, with an oar in its hand;
On the tide and the wave he was quickly afloat,
With no baggage to bother in the ferryman's boat.
Whene'er I see a poor man kneel,
  And hear his fervent, humble prayer,
Within my very heart I feel
  'Tis well that I am listening there.
Although to me his aims are dim,
That service may be much to him;
It tells of hopes beyond the screens—
  Of strugglings through a bitter strife,
Of trustings to an Arm unseen—
  Of outlooks to a higher life;
Whate'er my careless tongue may say,
My heart says—"let the poor man pray."

You see how oft my Muse will turn,
  And meet you with a smile or frown;
And imitate the old dash churn,
  That's either up or down.

Say, what would you give for a look
Through a book,
Containing each word from the lips of a human,—
In his billing and cooing,
In his efforts at wooing
The heart of a woman,
Since Adam first plucked up the courage to lead on,
And court that old girl in the garden of Eden?
When my hurry is over, with a plenty of time,
I am going to write such a volume in rhyme.

Though the record declares Adam took, as his bride,
Blushing Eve as she leaped from the rib in his side;
But the facts being known—oh, I think, 'twould be found,
That he courted her first when the Lord wasn't 'round.
He's a fool who would marry an angel of light,
Till he courted that angel at least for a night.
There was sense in the speech of the boy, who, you know,
Wouldn't work till he first got the hang of his hoe.
Ah! the first couple on the Eden ground—
What a big time they must have had in wooing—
No old folks standing tip-toe, "harking" 'round,
Nor "peeking" in to see what they were doing;
No foreign force to tempt them on to sin,
For this was just before the snake came in,

And Adam, to secure his female treasure,
Had the full swing around about in Asia;
And ere he dressed him in those fig-leaf pants,
Had elbow room that I had not at Grant's;
One thing looks queer, that they could not refrain
From hooking pears, and then from raising Cain.

How oft I dreamed through my young brains,
That I should lead in golden chains
My blushing, fair Almira,
As led that famed and warring man—
The Emperor Aurelian,
When, meeting with success one day,
He conquered proud Zenobia,
The Queen of old Palmyra.

The old folks woke when I sung "Brave Wolfe,"
Then kept a hem and hawing,
And then I let her "chaw" my gum,
Which I had just been "chawing."
I felt it like old Bible proof—
Her love was most divine—
When buckling down, with cherry lips,
She sucked the gum from mine.
But time has taught my cheated heart

To watch the smile and frown,
And see if it is love or gum
When woman buckles down;
For woman is woman wherever you go,
'Mid the jabbering hordes of the Esquimaux,
Or your lettered tribes, where the pearly face
Shows the tint of the Anglo Saxon race.
She snickered, and she chawed the gum,
When I hauled from my waist-coat,
And played my jewsharp I had bought
One day of Reuben Prescott.
Now, Prescott, since he sold that harp,
Much money has been clearing;
While I slopped over into rhymes,
He went to auctioneering.

We then played two of those old games
I learned of Esther Norris;
She beat me bad at fox and geese,
But I beat her at morris.
I told her how our old gray mare
Was getting lame and heavey;
'Twas one we had the Fall before
Of dickering Reuben Seavey.
Not Seavey—Maine's famed surgeon, now—

Not Calvin, I am sure—
Who learned to cut off legs and heads
Of the famed Scotch McRuer.

She then brought on some ivy leaves,
Just picked near Deacon Howse's—
We sat and sat, and ate the best,
And then we filled up, with the rest,
Both pockets of my trousers.

While I was sitting by her side,
And my new knife was showing—
She told me how that Peter Rich
With Dora Nutt was going.
She showed me her new calfskin shoes,
Her work-bag, and her duster—
Her vandyke and her green calash,
Which she had bought for muster.

Those calfskin shoes had turned up toes
She said, that one who knew her,
Told her to wear those turned up toes,
As they were more becoming to her.

Almira's wardrobe, or trousseau,
Was not like Butler's girl's, you know—
That rigging with those awful names,
Blanche wore when marrying General Ames.

All trimmed their gowns, with poppy leaves,
The girls we loved, in those old days—
They wore no modern "angel sleeves,"
With smilax and japonicas.

I had no extra clothes to show—
No satinet nor shoddy ;
But always hung all wardrobe then
On my voluptuous body.

The bull's-eye watch, her father clean
Had made by horses swapping,
To witness well the amorous scene,
Would now and then keep stopping.

Then hurrying up, with all its power,
Laid—while we both were fawning—
Its brassy hands upon the hour
Which told the birth of morning.

The rosy tints which fell aslant,
  And set the east aglowing,
Told me, if not Almira Grant,
  'Twas time that I was going.

Outside the door, on that blest morn,
  When heaven's blue stars were beaming,
Our first, pure, rustic kiss was born,
  While Shubael Grant lay dreaming.

In wending to my cottage home,
  The earth beneath and heavens above,
And all the circling spheres around,
  Bespoke and breathed of nought but love.

Andromeda, I noticed then,
  From the northern hemisphere,
Looked down and smiled, tho' chained behind
  Her mother, Cassiopea.

When they, and all the laughing hosts,
  Along the starry trail,
Reached out and fixed an extra kink
  In Ursa Major's tail.

When twilight's sable curtain falls,
  Then stars stand thick at even,
To act as outside sentinels
  Around the gates of heaven.

That night, along the shimmering slant—
  I tell you true, my brother—
The password was "*Almira Grant*"
  They whispered to each other.

The northern lights so leaped and flashed,
  And shot their fitful rays,
I thought that "long John" Couillard's shop
  One moment was ablaze.

And Boreas, bumming through the trees,
  Hushed up its mournful sigh,
And tried to laugh, like Shubael Grant
  Each time he told a lie.

I milked our cross, old lop horn cow—
  She never acted half so nice;
She never broke her bow but once,
  And never kicked my pail but twice.

Before that hour, a hook or kick
  Would follow up the slightest stir;
I think the love that fired my breast
  Wrought out that blessed change in her.

For every word from human lips,
  The harshest, kindest, and the least,
Will make its impress, deep and broad,
  Upon the heart of man or beast.

And not one thought sweeps o'er the soul,
  Though never by a word expressed,
But that some hovering spirit, round,
  Transfers it to another's breast.

And there, within its secret depths,
  So surely, steadily, though so still—
It toils through many a weary hour,
  And does its work for good or ill.

Had I this tough, old world to rule,
  My cannon, sword and mallet
Should be the dear old district school,
  God's Bible, and the ballot.

If Bible, ballot, and the school,
  Should fail me all, in turn, then let
Me have—instead of rabble rule—
  The educated bayonet.

Amid the tumult and the strife,
In weaving out our web of life,
Although the task be light or hard,
Whatever be the cost per yard—
  A doubloon or a shilling,
Regardless of our prayer or ban,
God furnishes the warp for man,
  But man must find the filling.

My Muse oft seeks some dizzy height,
  By giving one unearthly bound—
Then, quick as thought, she loves to light,
  And sing her songs on level ground.

Her folks, not mine, were well to live,
  And had a high position—
Though bed-quilts hanging up, they used
  Instead of board partition.

We had no boards to make two rooms,
  In hot or chilly weather,
And quilts we used on little groups
  That snuggled down together.

For mother's tear-stained widow's weeds
  To ten young hearts were telling,
That father could not toil for us
  In the land where he was dwelling.

To tell the honest truth, sometimes
They find these faults about my rhymes:
They say I use the pronoun I
Too often in my poetry,
  And given too much to blowing;
But then these facts you all should know—
  Two facts quite worth your knowing—
That pronoun *I* cannot be beat,
  Stand, speak it out as many times
  As I have used it in these rhymes,
And every time how full and sweet
Its echo strikes your ear-hole drum,
Which doctors call the tympanum.
Again, when earthly force was tried.
And man was humbled in his pride,

By aid of unseen spirit power—
Such as I feel this very hour—
The stern old walls of Jericho
  Were toppled once by blowing!

'Tis many a year since the old folks, mine,
  With their mortal eyes have seen us,
For their sight grew dim on a winter's day,
And they wandered off, and they lost their way;
But they pressed along, though they hardly knew
Which way to turn or what to do—
For the night came on and it chilled them through;
But I learn from a friend, who has just come back,
That they struck at last on a beaten track,
Which led the old folks safely o'er
To a fairer sky and a better shore,
  Though a mist now broods between us.
And my friend who has brought these tidings o'er
From that milder sky and the better shore,
Brings a word from the old folks living there,
Where the lands are green and the skies are fair,
We had better come, and we needn't fear,
For the work isn't hard, as the work is here,
And they have a home which they own all clear—
Not a mortgaged home as their home was here—

5

But a home as good as a home need be,
With a plenty of room for the girl and me.
And they sent me word, as they chanced to look
One day, in an old, worn spirit book,
Which the angels keep for the oath and prayer—
They found these words written out up there:
"Those chains which bind her as the wife
"To him within the lower land,
"Shall, by the laws of spirit life,
"Prove only as a rope of sand.

"For, after earth's mistakes are past,
"Each human, yearning, unmatched heart,
"In some of God's wide spheres at last
"Shall find its own true counterpart."

They told me, from those climes above,
One boon survives this mortal breath,
For there the beauteous form of love
Finds entrance through the gates of Death.

I have my child—a prattling girl—
One tie that binds me to my wife;
With laughing eyes and glossy curl—
A chip cut from my tree of life;

And long before her soul is fired
  By dreams of bridal ring and kiss,
I shall, perhaps, get worn and tired,
  And seek some other clime than this.
But then—what then? I'll take no sphere,
  Nor hidden place above, below,
Where I can gain no hint from here,
  To tell me how home matters go.
And should I learn my child's astray,
By flinging her young heart away,
Worse than the fate the Tuscan found,
Who to the rotting corpse was bound,
I swear by Him who gave me breath,
There is no secret power in death,
Nor force above which angels know,
Nor chains within the gulfs below,
Nor distance in the realms of God,
To keep me from my darling Maude!
I will come back by sign or grip,
By rap, or scroll, or table tip,
Or steal your human throngs among,
And seize upon some mortal tongue,
And warn my child to shun the deck,
The voyage with him—the storm—the wreck!

The story of my creed is brief,
I have this shadowy belief—
My only hope of real bliss—
That sometime, on some distant day,
I shall with penitential tear,
Find chance to blot or wash away,
Or, at the least, one chance to try
To palliate, or rectify,
Within some far more favored sphere,
Some blind mistakes I've made in this,
And not let Innocence atone
For crimes or errors of my own.

Don't get alarmed at my poet dreams,
At my ghostly, ghastly spirit themes,
For it may be in the times afar,
When spirit stocks are up at par,
I shall sell out, for here I own,
In the sight of Him on the great white throne,
In my wanderings 'round from creed to creed,
In my dashings off, at a fearful speed,
With my bark afloat on a doubtful wave,
To a fitful light beyond the grave;
I have learned no prayer that has seemed to me
Like the one I lisped at my mother's knee.

Fate has decreed, to win our wives
We cannot sail around their coop,
And come the night-hawk, when he dives,
And take them at a single swoop.

You cannot seize our modern dames,
With rings and bustles, hoops and curls—
As, at those Neptune feasts and games,
The Romans grabbed the Sabine girls.

But man must have his hours of fuss—
Must fawn and bluster, fret and crone,
In keeping off some rival "cuss,"
Who has more bear's-oil and cologne.

If you wish to out-do a Chinaman—
A real Chinaman to beat—
The safest, wisest, surest plan,
Is an extra braid in your flaunting queue;
In your vest an extra shade or two—
And an extra breadth in your trousers' seat;
And, my friend, if you ever fall in love,
And another is after your turtle-dove—
The safest, wisest, surest plan,
Is the same you would try on a Chinaman;

For woman is woman, wherever you go,
'Mong the jabbering hordes of the Esquimaux,
(Which I roamed among long years ago)
Or your lettered tribes, where the pearly face
Shows the tint of the Anglo Saxon race.

Since the primeval birth of morn,
When the voice came—"let there be light,"
There never was a woman born—
A real woman, moulded right,
Who would not, through this vale of tears,
Form one blade of the human shears.

Miss Katie Field you all must know,
That pure young type of womanhood—
I'll bet my head—worth much to me—
That Katie Field—yes, even she,
When in the Adirondack wood,
And for the night was snuggled down
Beside the soul of old John Brown;
Would sometimes dream about a beau—
A beau, not of the spirit form,
But clothed in solid flesh, so warm—
With sinewy arms to chop or hug,
With arms her kindling stuff to lug,

To build her fire and cook her food,
Within the Adirondack wood.
Experience proves 'twill never pay,
  To hire your wandering spirit bands,
  With boneless feet and nerveless hands,
To chop your cord-wood by the day.

Our bridal tour was all arranged—
  'Twas not for Saratoga,
Nor Orchard Beach, nor Belfast Bay—
Down where I caught a wife one day—
  And where they catch the porgy;
Nor Plymouth Rock, nor Mount Desert—
That natural place to fish and flirt—
But, then, as Grant's whole team and ours
  Were hauling bark for Skinner,
We 'greed to foot it down to Tower's,
  And wait till after dinner:—
Then take the bark road out by Wright's,
And stop with Betsey Cook two nights;
For Grant's own cousin, Peter Brooks,
Was shaving shingles down at Cook's.
In case the Cooks were not at home,
  Or didn't ask us both to stay,
We were to foot it back, that night,

And eat our sweet-cake on the way.
In a tough, hard old world like this,
'Twere well, if many more would be
Much like Almira Grant and me,
And guard against contingencies.
And then, to close our honey moon,
When she had knit some linen lace,
We were to spend one after-noon
At that old classic watering place
You all must know, that Lombard stream,
Where Dole, and Drew, and Booth and Locke
Caught suckers by the birch-bark gleam,
And where they watered all their stock.

Grant talked of adding to his house—
To make the rude log cabin square—
So, through my brain these thoughts would run,
When the dear girl and I were one,
With the first bran new Hampden stove,
With spread and tick her mother wove,
And chest, which Shubael Grant could make,
To keep our handsome clothes and cake,
And the whole mulberry tea-set bought
With blackberries the dear girl had got,
With six red chairs, all bottomed fine,

With basket stuff or "*ellum rine;*"
With blushing flowrets peeping through
The barrel we could saw in two;
With half-high bed and cedar broom,
We'd occupy the new front room,
  And take such solid comfort there.
God never made a purer gem,
That sparkles in a diadem,
Than the ambitious, modest pride,
Within the breast of the young bride,
Who strives—though poverty her lot—
To beautify her humble cot.

When you have loved some red-cheek girl,
With many a dimple, many a curl,
And waited on her night and day,
And many a side-comb given away,
  With heart and soul aglowing with her—
When Love has formed its choicest plan,
To find some short-legg'd gentleman,
  With frizzled hair, a going with her,
Although by nature meek and mild,
It makes you feel a little riled.

From saint or sinner, fop or prude,
There's nothing like pure gratitude.

For one I go, if I go alone,
For the sergeant, Tillman Joy,
Who told them square down at Spunky Point,
In the State of Illinois—
If they drove him out or they touched one hair
Of the black boy, Banty Tim,
Who trumped death's ace at the Vicksburg heights—
Yes, trumped death's ace for him;
When the sergeant told how his ribs caved in,
From the whirl of a splintered shell,
And the black boy shouldered and lugged him through,
From the fire-proof, gilt-edged hell;
How he stronged him off in his brawny arms,
At the ring of the Union calls,
Though his dark hide looked like a pepper-box,
As 'twas riddled by Rebel balls;
Yes, I go for these tough, rough words that boiled
From the heart of that sergeant Joy—
"He will rassle his hash in hell to-night
Who touches that black-skin boy!"

Fix all your earthly plans so nice,
And Burns would say—
"The best laid schemes o' mice an' men
Gang aft a-gley."

Another fellow gazed on her—
  A swanking, brainless high-head—
With this advantage over me,
  He'd better clothes than I had.

He wore a full-cloth suit of clothes,
  One made by a man tailor;
My mother made mine out of wale,
  Though cut by Hannah Kaler.

My home-made cap was red and blue,
  The young sprout seemed to chuckle,
For a felt hat graced his bullet head,
  With hat-band and with buckle.

The shirt I wore my mother made,
  Without much extra stitching,
'Twas carded, colored, spun and wove
  Within the old log kitchen.

He wore an eight cent boughten one—
  Though very few could use 'em,
And then, by thunder! in that shirt
  He had a linen bosom!

'Twas ironed stiffer than a stake—
He knew such bosom pleases—
And then 'twas ironed up and down,
And then across in creases.

And Cale had collar-buttons, too,—
My shirts I used to pin them;
And, don't you think, his wristbands once
Had bone sleeve-buttons in them!

His stocking yarn, he said, was dyed
By Mrs. Jonas Warner—
But mine was dipped in our own dye-house,
The dye-pot in the corner.

He used fresh bear's oil on his hair,
To please that mother's daughter;
I used a wooden pocket comb,
Dipped into soap and water.

'Mid all attempts to please the fair,
I think I never yet
Stuck side-combs in my parted hair,
Or wore a chemisette.

I have a love for things Divine,
  And every thing that's human—
Except a brothy female man,
  Conceived by a male woman.

I dined on bannocks at the school
  Kept down at Huldah Grover's;
He carried nut-cakes once a week,
  And frequently turnovers.

My hair was parted at the side—
  His parted in the middle;
I played upon the old bass drum—
  He played upon the fiddle.

Our buskin strings were made of tow,
  And twisted by each mother;
But after Caleb put on airs,
  His buskin strings were leather.

How many things like buskin strings,
  While travelling to death's portals,
Have builded high the walls of caste,
  To separate poor mortals!

He used a pongee handkerchief,
Lent by his cousin Hannah—
I used the one I carry now,
A cotton, red bandanna.

My fair-haired younger brother Lew.,
Was neither shoed nor booted,
But learning *then* to stump New York,
By stumping 'round barefooted.

I rubbed cold tallow on my shoes,
To keep those shoes from cracking;
On week days he used melted grease,
And Sundays he used blacking.

And both of Caleb's ears were bored—
A pegging awl run through them—
And two new German silver rings,
Like drops of sweat hung to them.

Some women cannot stand such show—
The gay "cuss" seemed to know it;
And so he spoiled one heaven-made match—
But made one earthly poet.

"*Poeta nascitur non fit*"
Was true, perhaps, when it was said,
But times, since then, have changed a bit;
For now-a-days, 'tis plain to see,
To save the nurse and doctor's fee,
Most poets are not born, but made.

Ah, vain attempt on me to try
The doctrine that there is no lie,
As some have sung or said;
That falsehood is the child of truth,
That capers 'round within its youth,
And stands upon its head.
I say it in this world beneath,
Yes, shout it in the very teeth
Of philosophic cant,
It was a whopper—nothing more—
That teetered me, in days of yore,
Out of Almira Grant.
You'll always find the road up hill
To drive one woman 'gainst her will;
Yes, even if you know most,
'Tis better, safer, to engage
To split wood with an iron wedge,
And drive it butt end foremost.

I promised to be true as steel,
  She promised to be truer—
But oaths she broke and 'came the bride
  Of fancy Cale McCluer.

Yes, ere twelve circling, golden suns
  Within the east had risen,
To fill my youthful cup with woes,
Both stood up in their handsome clothes,
And pressed each other's palms in turn,
He swearing ever to be "hern"—
  She swearing to be "hisen."

Cale cut me out and took the girl
  I loved and spotted for my wife;
But there are things besides the girls
  Of which we're oft cut out in life.

But, after all is done and said,
  'Tis better, as the heart will prove,
To love a girl you cannot wed,
  Than wed a girl you cannot love.

And though life's fiery trials bring
  Some vain regrets and bitter tears,

This earth is but a scaffolding—
A scaffolding so broad and grand—
On which God's spirit workmen stand,
To build us up for higher spheres.

One day Van Pronk, a Dutchman, died—
His widow, fair and good,
Ordered a likeness of Van Pronk—
A statue, carved from wood.

But soon another Dutchman came,
A Dutchman fresh and yonk;
The widow, for a courting fire,
Then split up old Van Pronk!

Almira, once of me so fond,
When Caleb came to woo her,
Split me, Van Pronk, for kindling wood,
To warm up Cale McCluer.

And such is life—both sons and sires,
The worldling and the monk—
To feed the flames of new desires,
Will split up old Van Pronk.

The Leathers's took up the cry,
And prophesied that I should die;
But, then, 'tis my belief
'Tis mighty seldom that you see
A gentleman built just like me
For standing love and grief.

We had no lawyer in our town
To take our greenbacks from us;
No learned man to bring, for me,
A suit for breach of promise.

These were long years before my mind
Had turned to legal reading—
Though 'Mira thought I understood
The forms of "special pleading."

So there are times when human laws
Cannot be found to save us;
We have to use those substitutes
Which God or Nature gave us.

Next day I mot the festive lover,
When Caleb put on airs anew—
When wounded love and wounded pride,

When anger and ambition, too,
Came rushing, frantic, to my side,
And fired the feelings of a man—
Then raised my double-sole brogan
Against the form of Cale McCluer—
That ponderous part of him, I'm sure,
Which seemed the most exposed to be—
That part of his anatomy,
Which gentlemen with coat-tails cover.
I felt it, whether wrong or right,
The hour had come for me to fight;
I felt myself in the same fix
As the old Massachusetts Six,
When, thro' the mob they hewed their way,
'Mid the first spatter of the gore—
Upon that wild, old April day—
In the red streets of Baltimore.
'Tis settled well; there seems to be
(I learn it from zoology)
Four types or grades of animals,
And which the man of science calls
The vertebrated,
Articulated,
The mollusk,
And the radiated.

That day, in looking Caleb over,
I found the festive rival lover
  Possessed the functions of the four;
But when I raised my foot to route him,
  I found,—
  The way he measured off the ground—
There was but little man about him.
With my passions boiled down in my youthful brogan,
Oh, the way that I routed that young married man
Makes me think of the time, on that glorious day,
That we routed the Rebs in the Winchester fray;
When Phil. Sheridan flew o'er the Winchester course—
Resembling the picture of Death on his horse.
If there's one in this crowd, to the Union so true,
That he shouldered his gun, and was dressed up in blue,
And was there in that fight—in that battle so grand—
I will wait for a time till he holds up his hand;—
Yes, I see you were there, when the old starry flag
Slapped its folds in the face of that rattle-snake rag.
  Bret Harte, no doubt, in writing how poor Walker
    Was dogged from rock to tree,
  Had heard about my routing Cale McCluer,
    And took his style from me.
  Bret says, when Walker blew a hole thro' Peters,
    For telling him he lied—

Then up and dusted out of South Hornitos,
  Across the long Divide;
They ran out at Strong's, and up thro' Eden,
  And 'cross the ford below;
Then up the mountain—Peters' brother leadin'—
  With guide, and Clark, and Joe.

I feel it, somehow,
That I ought to be a little more definite now,
And to tell you the spot, on this new married man,
That I hit with the sole of my maddened brogan;
It was just at the forks that was made by his pins,
  And near at the point—if my memory don't fail—
  Where Agassiz tells me the base of the tail
Of a perfectly well formed gorilla begins.
As age creeps on, 'tis strange how memory fails—
For, come to think, gorillas have no tails!
Another blind mistake, 'twixt you and me,
I never saw this famous Agassiz.
One sterling principle of law
  I find is settled well—
Each has the right to run or fight,
  In earth, or heaven, or hell;
But cannot find, in any code,
The Koran, Shaster, or the Word

Which Moses from the mountain heard;
In any musty book of mine—
The human, doubtful, or Divine—
  'Tis written down a sin
To gently raise your young brogan
Against the form of any man,
Who steals by night your girl away—
Then puts on airs the coming day,
  And tries to rub it in.

Cale's father kept a dancing school—
  Perhaps the old folks, present, knew him—
He was a fiddling barber, too;
  His wife was double cousin to him.
They say when double cousins wed,
  By Fowler's phrenologic rules,
Their children are almighty smart,
  Or else they are almighty fools.
Now Caleb spread himself so wide
  He lapped each phrenologic rule;
For, every day and every time,
  Cale was a smart almighty fool.
On marriages I make no raids;
I make no thrusts at honest trades;
By sledge and hammer, spade and hoe,

By lathered brush or rosined bow,
By sword and lancet, pill and probe,
By priestly cowl and priestly robe;
  Man has the right to earn his pelf—
Although, from policy or pride,
I keep no striped pole outside,
By razors strapped on Coke and Kent,
And lather made from twelve per cent.,—
  I run a shaving mill myself!
But then, amid my wrong and right,
  I never did nor never can
Defraud a fool, a cripple fight,
  Or plague a crazy man.
But then, this fact you all should know,
  Though made from decent metals,
I think, before that I should go
  Ten days without my victuals,
And could not beg or buy a meal—
E'en pride would show me how to steal.

I've read—but where I cannot say—
  In that old Indian book by Drake,
In Hudibras or Rabelais,
Or else, perhaps, in Ida May,
  Or dreamed it all when wide awake;

In Audubon on forest birds,
Or Ganssen's Plenary Inspiration;
In Doctor Dadd on flocks and herds,
Or Rollin on some ancient nation;
In some weird tale by Walter Scott,
His Black Dwarf or his Quentin Durward;
In Mrs. Lane's Forget-Me-Not,
Or those etherial songs by Sherwood—
In some old book where gibberish words
Were found like "*ego, tuus, meus*,"
Or in some work of modern date,
Your Ecce Homo, Ecce Deus;
In Random Rambles 'Mong the Tombs,
Which make the brain feel wild and frantic;
In some quaint scrap by Wendell Holmes,
Just published in the last Atlantic;
In Miracles by Doctor Stone,
Or rhymes by Hosea Bigelow,
Or Uncle Tom by Mrs. Stowe;
Hold up your horses; here I own
I've given these names just for a show,
As thousand others have before,
To make the auditors—the green—
Believe they have a world of lore
From books their eyes have never seen.

I never read one-half the books
  Here named, so pompously, to-night;
And, ten to one, 'twixt me and you,
  I havn't spelt the names aright.
I have no eye, no love—I own—
  For beauties in your lettered lore,
Upon the cold, white leaf alone
  I find no heart to look them o'er;
But let those lettered beauties shine
Upon this brain and heart of mine,
  All pure and radiant, fresh and warm,
Shine through that strange, mysterious prism;
  Some human, *sympathetic* form,
But yet *intenser* organism;
  Or held within that circling band,
Upon the unseen verging line
  Which separates the border land;
And I can see and feel their power,
And in the fervent, frenzied hour,
Transfer those rays with rustic art
Which fall upon my brain and heart.

Now let me stop and quote eight lines
  From Lalla Roo, or Lalla Rookh,
You'll find the verses printed out

In Tom Moore's Irish poet book:
"Oh, ever thus, from childhood's hour,
"I've seen my fondest hopes decay—
"I never loved a tree or flower,
"But 'twas the first to fade away.
"I never nursed a dear gazelle,
"To glad me with its soft black eye,
"But when it came to know me well,
"And love me, it was sure to die."

Moore wrote those lines with heart and soul,
With thought some critic's taste to please;
But, writing them, Tom felt no worse
Than I, in writing lines like these.

A pale thin form oft meets my gaze,
Clad out in tattered dresses,
Compelled to take, through forms of law,
A bloated brute's caresses.

And, as she passes, oft I dream
When in my office lawing,
That form resembles a green girl
That my spruce gum was "chawing."

And, ah! I well remember once,
In making up my docket,
Instead of my old client's name—
I think his name was Patrick Dunn—
My hand, entranced, wrote out the name,
The strangely magic name of one
Who, by a tallow candle's light,
Crammed ivy leaves with me, one night,
Into my trousers' pocket.

Oh, for that blessed hour and place,
When some benign divinities
May furnish souls, unmated here,
With spiritual affinities!

I care not where that place may be,
Though to that place is given
The common scare-crow name of hell,
Or the milder one of heaven.

How, many and many an hour, I feel
That Cale McCluer should meet my steel,
Or whizzing bullet, were it not
For this truth that Hans Breitmann wrote:
"Ach, de efils dat from efil

"Troo a life ish ever grow!
"Had I never dink I killed you
"Many a man were livin now—
"Many a man dat shleeps in canebrakes,
"Many a man py pillow-shore;
"For dy morder mate me reckelos,
"And *von* tead man gries for more!"

I have, upon life's lower plane,
Some darling ones around me;
And I have ties, in upper spheres,
Whose spirit links have bound me;
And I have bread enough in store,
And friends, from judge to peasant,—
To keep the gaunt wolf from my door,
At least just for the present.
I love them all as man should love,
And love to write and sing 'em,
But since that strange and primal brush
Which came from that girl's gingham;
My heart has never beat as then,
While sitting by Almira,
Upon that night I reckon from
As Arabs from Hegira.

'Tis said the microscope now tells
  That every breathing human frame
Is made from little curious cells,
  And all too numerous to name;
That each contains distinct, alone,
A life, a being of its own.
Oh, could I be but young once more!
  I feel I can, then feel I can't—
And she were blooming as of yore—
  That daughter of old Shubael Grant;
How would my spirit love to dwell,
For ages, in each tiny cell,
Then garner in each little life,
And form one entity—a wife;
I ask no purer draught of bliss—
No other Moslem heaven than this:
Except outside my gate I should
Keep Cale McCluer sawing wood.
I went to Denmark once, you know,
And there I learned that, years ago,
In Jutland, when a warrior died,
  They took the mailed and grinning corse,
And stretched the stiffened legs astride
  The back of his scarred battle horse,
Then pranced the snorting steed around,

When the pale corse
And the live horse
Were buried 'neath some burial mound.
I cannot help it—no, I can't—
When thinking of Almira Grant;
I sometimes wish I was that corse,
If Cale McCluer was my horse!

With all my love for Caleb's bride,
Of one thing I am sure,
Though you may take my pledge or not,
I will not on this earthly side
Lay claim by act, or word, or thought,
To the wife of Cale McCluer.
Maine's statute law gives Cale the right
To claim that wife both day and night;
But may be, on that yonder side—
That spirit side the water—
Where old earth laws are all repealed,
And truth and love are quick revealed,
As Cale McCluer did years ago,
I may just put on airs, you know,
And ask the curl haired spirit fop
To vacate, there, his bridal shop,
And then take charge of Caleb's wife.
And of old Shubael's daughter.

The new-born, blissful butterfly,
While scooting through the liquid sky,
  With its etherial tiller,
May recollect, and with a squirm,
The way folks used him when a worm,
  Or creeping caterpillar.
Though arms be swapped for wings, yet I
May think back like the butterfly;
  "For time at last sets all things even,
"And, if we do but watch the hour,
"There never yet was human power
  "Which could evade, if unforgiven,
"The patient search, and vigil long,
"Of him who treasures up a wrong."

But you may quickly ask me how
I'll manage her I live with now?
To tell you, truthfully and plain,
The way she blows me, now and then,
And calls me fool so many a time,
When mumbling o'er some love-sick rhyme,
I'm not so sure, that even she
Would not be glad to dicker me
  For spirit Cale McCluer,
When freed from earth, and fairly o'er

Upon the untried misty shore;
For Cale, though here a noted curse,
Has never writ one love-sick verse.

But I have blabbed of death enough—
I feel the risk of death like this:
'Tis like the playing blindman's bluff
Around some fearful precipice.
All creeds and all foundations laid,
All promises through pardoning grace,
Are swept like grass before the blade,
When gazing in a dead man's face.

"There is not of that castle gate,
"Its draw-bridge or portcullis weight,
"Stone, bar, moat, bridge or barrier left,
"Nor of its fields a blade of grass,
"Save what grows on a ridge of wall
"Where stood the hearth-stone of the hall."

Thus spoke the old Mazeppa, freed
From Palestine's wild Tartar steed;
And thus speak I, that you may know
The fate of Grant's old log house, where
McCluer and I, long years ago,
Once battled for Almira there;

That castle to which Caleb ran,
With three hoists from my young brogan.

The cot where Shubael Grant once dwelt
  Has felt the force of Time's decay,
The place where 'Mira's mother knelt
  I visited but yesterday;—
I heard no sound like those of yore,
  When Grant's whole tribe of children played;
I found no foot-prints at the door,
  Which I or Cale McCluer made.
A groan, a tear—the spade, the mound—
  Then the tall grass came bending o'er
The forms of three young laughing girls,
  Who "peaked" down thro' that chamber floor.
Those three small boys, who cuddled down,
  Within the trundle-bed, that night,
Dressed up in blue and went to God
  From Spottsylvania's gory fight!
One topless tree now stands between
  Two knolls where Shubael piled his wood,
One little heap of rocks is seen,
  On which the catted chimney stood.
Around that spot how many a time,
  When dreaming, drunk with saddened bliss,

Some relic of a Scottish rhyme
  Has pelted at my heart like this:
    "My master's gone, and no one now
      "Dwells in the halls of Ivor,
    "Men, dogs and horses, all are dead—
      "I am the sole survivor."
When Cale McCluer had stole my girl,
  And brokers came one chilling morn,
And claimed, through my dead father's deed,
  My mother's cot, where I was born—
I cannot tell the reason why,
  But heart and brain and nerve grew strong,
And quickly took this wholesome hint
  From fragments of an Irish song:
    "When nettles grow around the hearth,
  And towers that now so stately stand,
    In scattered fragments fill the earth,
  And Saxon strangers own the land,
    To Adrighoole's sea-beaten coast—
  Then let O'Gara's son repair,
    Wealth far beyond what he has lost,
  And joy shall be restored him there."

CONCLUSION.

Now go to your homes, whether husband or wife,
With a hope in the skies and a purpose in life;
Tho' you revel in wealth, or thro' poverty plod,
Be true to yourselves, to each other, and God;
In your journeyings thro', whether servant or master,
Like the brave engineer at the Hamburg disaster—
Whatever your loss or whatever your gain—
Like immortal "Doc Simmons," *go down with the train.*"

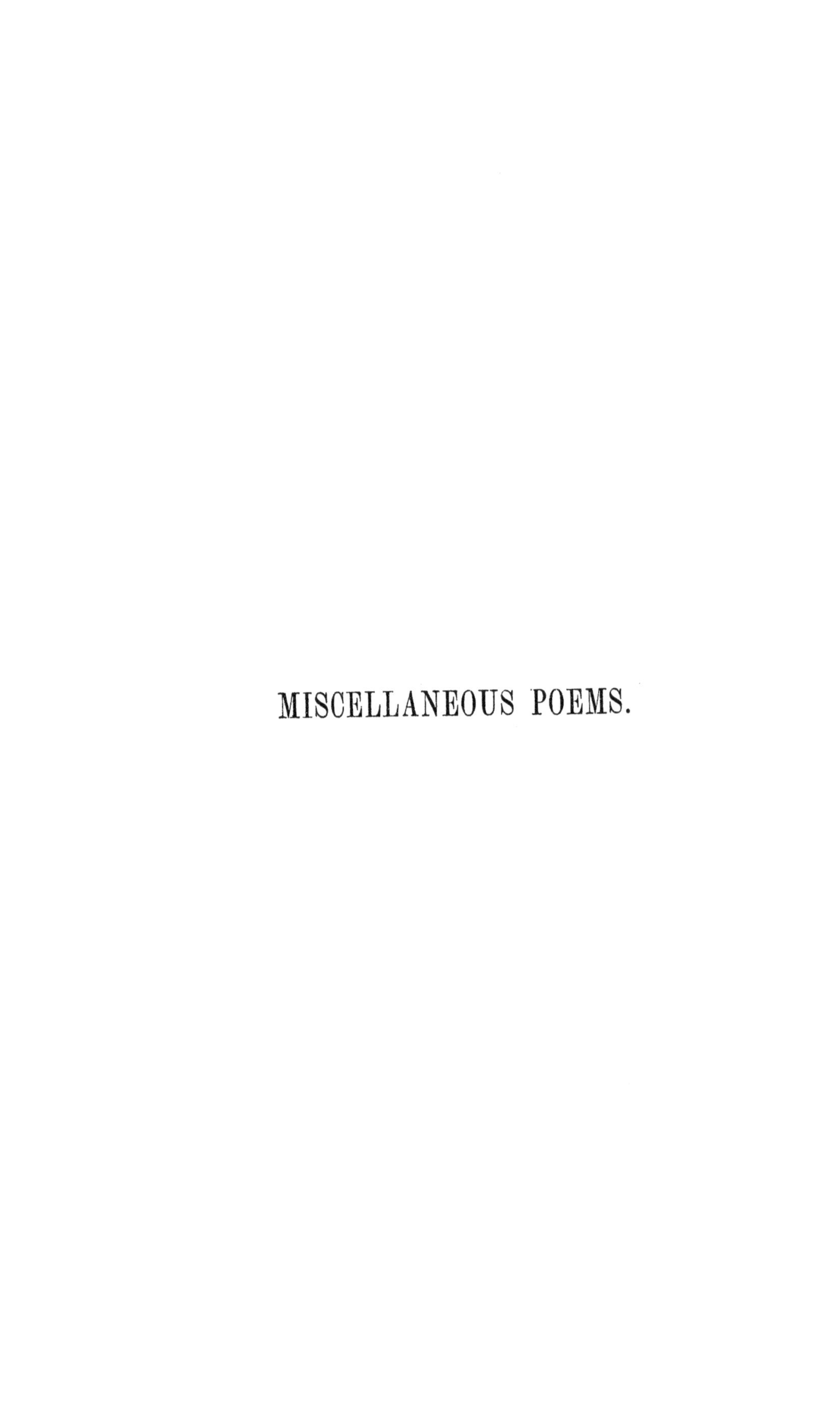

MISCELLANEOUS POEMS.

THE UNDER DOG IN THE FIGHT.

I know that the world—that the great big world—
From the peasant up to the king,
Has a different tale from the tale I tell,
And a different song to sing.

But for me, and I care not a single fig
If they say I am wrong or am right,
I shall always go in for the weaker dog,
For the under dog in the fight.

I know that the world—that the great big world—
Will never a moment stop
To see which dog may be in the fault,
But will shout for the dog on top.

But for me—I never shall pause to ask
Which dog may be in the right—
For my heart will beat, while it beats at all,
For the under dog in the fight.

Perchance what I've said, I had better not said,
Or, 'twere better I had said it *incog*,
But with heart and with glass filled chock to the brim,
Here is luck to the bottom dog.

THE SIGN OF DISTRESS.

'Twas a wild dreary night in the cheerless December,
'Twas a night only lit by a meteor's gleam;
'Twas the night of that night, I distinctly remember,
That my soul journeyed forth on the wings of a dream.

That dream found me happy, by tried friends surrounded,
Enjoying with rapture the comforts of wealth,
My cup overflowing, with blessings unbounded,
My heart fully charged from the fountains of health.

That dream left me wretched—by friendship forsaken,
Dejected, despairing, and wrapped in dismay,
By poverty, sickness and sorrow o'ertaken,
To every temptation and passion a prey,

In frenzy, the wine-cup I instantly quaffed at,
And habit and time made me quaff to excess,
But heated by wine, like a madman, I laughed at
The thought of e'er giving a Sign of Distress.

But wine sank me lower, by lying pretences,
It tattered my raiment and furrowed my face,
It palsied my sinews and pilfered my senses,
And forced me to proffer a Sign of Distress.

I reeled to a chapel where churchmen were kneeling,
And asking their Savior poor sinners to bless,
My claims I presented, the door of that chapel
Was slammed in my face at the Sign of Distress.

I strolled to the priest, to the servant of heaven,
And sued for relief with a wild eagerness;
He prayed that my *sins* might at last be forgiven,
And thought he had answered my Sign of Distress.

I staggered at last to the home of my mother,
Believing my prayers would meet with success;
But father, and mother, and sister and brother,
Disowned me, and taunted my Sign of Distress.

I lay down to die, as a stranger drew nigh me,
A spotless white lambskin adorning his dress,
My eye caught the emblem, and ere he passed by me,
I gave, as before, the sad Sign of Distress.

With Godlike emotions that messenger hastens
  To grasp me, and whisper, "my brother, I bless
The hour of my life when I learned of the Masons,
  To give and to answer your Sign of Distress."

Let a sign of distress by a Craftsman be given,
  And though priceless to me is eternity's bliss,
May my name never enter the records of heaven,
  Should *I* fail to acknowledge that Sign of Distress.

WHERE THE OLD FOLKS LIVED AND DIED.

I never shall tell who the old folks were,
  'Tis a wasting of time and breath,
To give you the names of the humble pair,
  Who have passed through the courts of death.

But the cot on the lot on the top of the hill,
  Near the spot where I just have cried—
'Tis the lot where the old folks toiled and lived,
  And the cot where the old folks died—

Is dearer far to my weary heart
  Than the dearest spot of earth,

For that was the cot on the lot on the hill
  Where the old folks gave me birth.

There's a slab near the cot on the lot on the hill,
  That will tell to the traveller there
When the old folks passed through the gates of death,
  And the names of the humble pair.

When I tire of the toils and the cares of my life,
  Oh, then, at the spot where I cried,
Near the cot let me sleep, on the top of the hill,
  Cuddled down by the old folks' side.

THE COVERED BRIDGE.

Tell the fainting soul in the weary form,
  There's a world of the purest bliss,
That is linked as that soul and form are linked,
  By a covered bridge with this.

Yet to reach that realm on the other shore,
  We must pass through a transient gloom,
And must walk unseen, unhelped, and alone,
  Through that covered bridge—the tomb.

But we all pass over on equal terms,
For the universal toll,
Is the outer garb, which the hand of God
Has flung around the soul.

Though the eye is dim, and the bridge is dark,
And the river it spans is wide,
Yet faith points through to a shining mount,
That looms on the other side.

To enable our feet, in the next day's march,
To climb up that golden ridge,
We must all lie down for a one night's rest,
Inside of the covered bridge.

GENERAL BERRY.*

Oh, wipe out the tears that bedim;
What! standing and weeping for him—

The soldier—why, this is not he
In the long, narrow box that you see.

* General Hiram G. Berry, of Rockland, was killed at the battle of Chancellorsville, May 3d, 1863, and buried with military and masonic honors at Rockland, May 14th, 1863; and the foregoing stanzas I wrote for the purpose of reading at the burial service, but was not able to attend.

He lives on just the same as before;
This is only the blouse that he wore—

That he wore 'mid the din and the strife,
In the terrible battle of life.

Though death, in his terrible raid,
Has stolen the sheath from his blade;

Yet that blade shall be witnessed again
In the fight, o'er the ranks of his men.

When yon waves, marshalled out like a host,
Shall forget to march up 'round your coast;

When these quarries beneath us shall fail,
And the sun and the moon shall turn pale;

When the stars shall wane out from the sky,
Then the name of your Berry shall die;

For he fell with a myriad like him,
Striking chains from the manacled limb.

Then dry up the tears that bedim;
Not standing and weeping for him—

The warrior—for this is not he
In the long, narrow box that you see.

THE POOR WOOD-HAULER.

Do you think of the forty years ago,
  When you and I were smaller,
And the cold, dead man that was found in the snow,
  Whom we'll call the poor wood-hauler?

With a manly heart, he was bartering wood
  From the home where love had bound him,
To deal with an honest hand the food
  To the flock that cuddled 'round him.

When that staff we leaned upon was broke—
  In that awful hour, my brother,
We had nothing left to lean upon,
  But God and a Roman mother.

But that mother's *form* is trembling now—
  Though her *spirit* is strong as ever—
An is tottering down, with a feeble step,
  To the banks of a stormy river.

Hark! I hear a voice o'er the river's roar—
  'Tis a voice that seems to call her—
And it comes from that man on the misty shore,
  Oh! I see—'tis the poor wood-hauler.

THE SHEPHERD AND THE LAMB.

In the Scottish hills, as a shepherd strolled,
On an eve, with his ancient crook,
He found a lamb that was chilled and young,
By the side of a purling brook.

And through fear that the lamb might sicken and die,
From its mother's side might roam,
He carried it up with a tender care,
To a fold in his highland home.

Mid the dreary night, o'er the cragged peaks,
Through the winds, and the storms, and the cold,
The mother followed her captured lamb
To the door of the shepherd's fold.

Once we had a lamb by its mother's side,
It was artless, and pure, and mild,
'Twas the dearest lamb in my own dear flock,
Oh, the pale, little blue-eyed child.

But a shepherd came, when the sun grew low,
By a path that has long been trod,
And he carried our lamb through the mists of night,
To his fold in the mount of God.

With a tearful eye, and a bleeding heart,
We must bear it and struggle on,
And climb that mount by the shepherd's track,
To the fold where our lamb has gone.

A WELCOME TO THE 2d MAINE REGIMENT.*

Though enfeebled by clime, and disfigured by scars,
Here's a "welcoming home" to you, children of Mars.

From your honors and perils, through your rivers of gore,
We will welcome you back like the Templars of yore.

Like the Knights who (the song and the legend hath told)
Brought their wounds from the lance of the Paynim of old.

We will welcome you, warriors, all weary and worn,
We will welcome your banners, all tattered and torn;

For those rents tell the world you've accomplished your part
And the light streaming through gilds the hope of the heart.

But I see through the lens of a glistening tear—
Oh, I see what my heart hath long taught me to fear;

* The Second Maine Regiment, under Colonel Varney, was received by the c authorities of Bangor, May 25, 1863, and I read the foregoing poem to them at Noro bega Hall.

There are some of your braves who walked out in their might—
There are some from your ranks, who went forth to the fight,

Are not here with you now, in a bodily form—
Are not here, in your ranks, with their hearts beating warm.

But they know and they feel, and they live as before—
'Mid your scenes of to-day they are here *en rapport.*

Though the check on your rolls makes a part of you slain,
Yet we welcome you all as the Second of Maine!

And to you who survive, and to those who have bled,
Here's a welcome to all, whether living or dead!

THE PALE BOATMAN.

In that cold and ancient wherry,
By that thronged, though fearful ferry,
O'er that bold and boisterous river,
See that Boatman, bending ever.

He has toiled for every nation
Since the birth-day of creation.

When old Eve, our primal mother,
Wiped the death-damp from Cain's brother,

Then that Boatman took that wherry,
And first crossed that fearful ferry;

Looked he stern and pale beside it,
At that first time that he tried it.

Mortals!
You and I must go in
That same boat which he is rowing!

THE OLD CAMP GROUND.

As the sun sank down to rest,
Like a child upon the breast,
Guarded by the picket on his round,
Each regiment and corps,
With another day's toil o'er,
Was feasting on the old camp ground.

But there came another sound,
For the grape and shot and shell—
Hissing like a fiend of hell—
On their serried columns fell;
At the closing of the fight,
In the darkness of the night,
There was blood upon the old camp ground.

Then the hasty, fervent prayer
Of the priest, who hurried there,
Like a mother kneeling o'er
Some young hero in his gore,
Faintly gasping out the name
That an absent loved one bore;
Told of who the wine-press trod,
Told of hope and faith in God,
To the dying on the old camp ground.

When the night had worn away,
Then the blessed beams of day,
By the spade and ditch and mound,
Told that spirits, brave and true,
Had forsook those forms in blue,
And ascended from the old camp ground.

TO "LEATHER FRENCH." *

You have haunted the dreams of my sleep,
Leather French,
You have troubled me often and long,
And so now to give rest to the waves of my soul,
Leather French, let me sing you a song.

* Stephen Y. French, a well-known hermit, called "Leather French," died at the almshouse in Exeter, March 8, 1858, aged about 80 years.

I suppose that the cold world may sneer,
Leather French,
For they've done it too often before,
When the innermost spirit has snatched up its harp,
Just to sing o'er the grave of the poor.

Never mind, let them laugh, let them sneer,
Leather French,
We will not be disturbed by them long,
For we'll step out aside from the battle of life,
While I question and sing you my song.

You were poor when you lived here below,
Leather French,
And you suffered from hunger and cold,
And 'twas well you escaped from the storm and the blast,
At the time you grew weary and old.

Has that old leather garb that you wore,
Leather French,
That you wore in the days long ago,
Been exchanged for the robe that you named in your prayer,
For a robe that is whiter than snow.

And that dreary old hut where you dwelt,
Leather French,
That old hut on the hurricane lands,

Was it bartered by you at the passes of death,
  For a house not erected with hands?

When the toys that I love become stale,
                    Leather French,
  And my life's fitful fever has passed,
Shall I safely cross over the Jordan of death,
  Shall I meet you in heaven at last.

Tell me true—tell me all—tell me now—
                    Leather French,
  For the tale you can tell me is worth
More to me than the wisdom, the pleasures, the fame
  And the riches and honors of earth.

Shall I meet no response to my call,
                    Leather French,
  Tell me *quick*, for I cannot wait long,
For I'm summoned again to the battle of life—
  Leather French—I have finished my song.

A SOLACE FOR DARK HOURS.

(Written in dark hours.)

A purling rill, so small and weak,
Once nearly died upon its way,
While running round the sea to seek,
Upon a summer's day.

But soon a cloud hung o'er that rill,
And soon came down an autumn rain,
When quick it danced by vale and hill,
Restored to strength again.

So pilgrim, though your cloud should lower,
Though sorrow's storm should come at length,
Yet God may clothe that storm with power,
To give your spirit strength.

It is not best that all should live
'Mid peaceful gales, 'neath sunny skies,
For cloud and tempest often give
Rich blessings in disguise.

The seaman's bark, whose bellied sail
The storm has drenched and wind has filled,
To reach its destined port might fail,
If storm and wind were stilled.

And thus our barks may quicker find,
Though long of angry waves the sport,
Though dashed ahead by storm and wind,
A final, peaceful port.

The smouldering coals that underneath
Some cumberous pile have calmly lain,
Might fire the world, if fanned by breath
Of passing hurricane.

And brother, now, perhaps thou hast,
Deep buried 'neath plebeian name,
A fire, which touched by sorrow's blast,
May kindle into flame.

The rust that creeps o'er warrior's blade,
When Peace can sleep without alarms,
Is seen no more, when shout is made:
"To arms!—the foe!—to arms!"

And thus a readiness for strife,
For *action* in this world of fight,
May both protect the spirit's life,
And keep its weapons bright.

How oft the fearful conflict seems
To weaken woe and strengthen weal,

By hardening up the softened nerves,
As smith-man hardens steel.

Fear not the man of wealth and birth,
Securely resting in his seat,
But sooner him, who, dashed to earth,
Is rising to his feet.

From straightened bow the arrowed spear,
By warrior's arm is never sent;
The danger which you have to fear,
Comes when that bow is bent.

MARY HALL.

My heart with grief is riven,
When I think of Mary Hall,
Though she dwells in yonder heaven,
If there is a heaven at all;
Yes, she died and went to heaven,
If there is a heaven at all.

The stars refused at night
To shine from out the skies,
When the mellow, liquid light
Floated forth from Mary's eyes;

When she lived, such liquid light
  Floated forth from Mary's eyes.

The modest flower and meek
  Always felt ashamed to bloom,
For the tint on Mary's cheek,
  Ere we laid her in the tomb,
Made the modest flower and meek
  Always feel ashamed to bloom.

The angels getting lonely
  In their old and quiet home,
Sent a word to Mary, only,
  Just for Mary Hall to come;
The word was, "Mary, only,
  None but Mary Hall to come."

The courier could not tarry,
  Only just to make the call,
So he threw a garb o'er Mary—
  'Twas a dark and funeral pall—
And he fled to heaven with Mary,
  If there is a heaven at all.

DIED:

At Exeter, (Maine) Emma, daughter of Francis W. and Sarah A. Hill, aged 14 years.

We have laid aside your casket,
Peacefully to rest,
With that simple wreath of flowers
Blushing on the breast;

While your mates, with tones of music,
'Round the casket stand,
Cheering on the trembling spirit
To the Morning Land.

For this pleasing, painful trouble,
For this tearful task,
Simple are the terms of payment—
Is the boon we ask.

From your home, which love inherits,
O'er this vale of tears,
With your choir of kindred spirits,
In those happier spheres—

On some beauteous Summer evening,
When the world is still,
Send us back those tones of music,
Angel Emma Hill.

ONLY SHE AND I.

Since our last, tho' rapturous meeting,
Years have flitted by,
Yet I mind it, how we met there—
Only she and I.

Quickly after that last meeting,
Life's embittered storm
Frightened out her trembling spirit
From its fragile form.

'Tis no matter—all no matter—
In God's future years
We shall meet again together,
Somewhere in the spheres.

When that meeting—how that meeting,
Where, I cannot say—
But I'm sure of such a meeting,
At no distant day.

Yes, within some cozy corner,
In the earth or sky,
We shall hold one blessed meeting—
Only she and I.

MY CHILD'S ORIGIN.

One night as old Saint Peter slept,
He left the door of heaven ajar,
When through a little angel crept,
And came down with a falling star.

One summer as the blessed beams
Of morn approached, my blushing bride,
Awakened from some pleasing dreams,
And found that angel by her side.

God grant but this, I ask no more,
That when he leaves this world of sin,
He'll wing his way for that blest shore,
And find the door of heaven again.

MY SISTER.

How calmly she sleeps in the grave,
    Let her rest;
How sadly the cypress trees wave
    O'er her breast.

How anxiously gazed I with fear,
    At her bed;
How startling the sound in my ear,
    "She is dead!"

What a night brooded over that day,
    What a gloom,
When bearing her slowly away
    To the tomb.

Let me live as she lived, and die
    As she died;
Deny me not this, let me lie
    At her side.

How sweetly we'll rest in the grave,
    When I die,
Though nought but the cypress trees wave
    Where we lie.

EARLY RECOLLECTIONS.

I'm sitting alone, in my office, dear Lew.,
  Both writing and singing my lays,
I'm laughing and crying, as memory runs back,
  To the time of our boyhood days.

Though lawyer you are, do you mind it, dear Lew.,
  The cottage where first we saw light,
Which father so carefully chinked up with moss,
  To keep all the crevices tight?

D'ye mind it, your lubberly form, my dear Lew.,
  Your eyes ever laughing through tears,
Your ball and your skates, and your trundling hoop,
  The bliss of your earlier years?

D'ye mind it, the times I have switched you, dear Lew.,
  When, "*Mother!*" or some such a shield,
Was the word that instinctively burst from your lips,
  While *I* took to the woods or the field?

D'ye mind it, the road with the gateway, dear Lew.,
  That led down to Stevens's mill—
The spot where old Patrick the porcupine slew,
  Near the "little great rock" on the hill?

D'ye mind it, our mother's red cupboard, dear Lew.,
  Where nut-cakes and bannocks were kept;
The old trundle-bed, that was pulled out on trucks,
  Where we have so peacefully slept?

At pic-nic and tavern and jam, my dear Lew.,
  I've feasted quite often, since then,
But all of such feasts I would give to the dogs,
  To lunch at that cupboard again.

Since then, upon mattress and sofa, dear Lew.,
  Oft times I have pillowed my head,—
But, ah, I have never yet found such repose
  As came from that old trundle bed!

Our mother, dear Lew., though decrepit and old,
  Has baked us a loaf, now and then,
To see if by practice we ever could find
  The tastes of our childhood again!

That poor mother's labors, I fear, were in vain,
  Our efforts were powerless, too,
For life's bitter emptings has tainted those loaves,
  And poisoned our appetites, Lew.

D'ye mind it, old Hephzibah's ferule, dear Lew.,
  Which taught us to read and to spell?

The fears of that ferule were kin to the fears
I now entertain of a hell.

That ferule was missing, one noon, my dear Lew.,
While Hephzibah went to her home,—
Ase Lombard—but Asa I will not expose—
For, mind it, we 'greed to keep mum.

D'ye mind it, our terrible punishment, Lew.,
That sitting with Catherine Russ!
Our peeping thro' fingers when prisoned there, too,
To see who were giggling at us?

'Tis strange, my dear Lew., how that habit, of late,
Has conquered that boyish fear;
Since then I have sat a whole night beside Kate,
Without even shedding one tear!

D'ye mind it, the place where we teetered, dear Lew.,
The fence that stood over the run?
Such teetering, Lew., was an innocent sport;
For, mind it, we teetered for fun.

Since then I have teetered with larger sized boys,
But always have teetered for pelf;
I've teetered full many a lad from the plank,
But once I got teetered myself.

D'ye mind it, the dreadful long night that we passed—
  The night we divided our coin—
The ninepence we saved for the muster, dear Lew.,
  The muster that came in the morn?

D'ye mind it, old Robinson's husking, dear Lew.,
  Where all drank new rum from a jug;
Where husking commenced with a jig and a reel,
  And closed with a kiss and a hug?

I am now a rigid teetotaller, Lew.,
  And stick to my principles snug,
And nothing would tempt me to "liquor" again,
  Unless 'twas old Robinson's jug!

D'ye mind it, how anxious you were, my dear Lew.,
  To have the good haying-time last
One season, when finding a bumble-bees' nest,
  In every rock-heap that you passed?

D'ye mind it, the day of all days in our youth,
  When death came so horrid and grim,
And brandished his scythe till he clipped the last thread
  Of the life of the dog we called "Prim?"

D'ye mind it, the knoll by the "beech-bars," dear Lew.,
  Where beech-nuts so many we got.

And lugged in our caps down to Huckins' store,
To barter for powder and shot?

Since beech-nuts grew *dull*, Lew, I've tried other schemes,
And now am in business that pays;
But all of my gains I would toss to the winds
For a month of our boyhood days.

For, mind it, those times were the times when we thought
What any one said must be true;
Since then, from some causes I will not explain,
A change has come over us, Lew.

If days like the days I am talking of, Lew.,
Through eternity's rounds could be given,
As true as my Bible I'd not give a fig
For a pass through the portals of heaven.

THE OLD SHIP OF STATE.

O'er the dark and the gloomy horizon that bounds her,
Thro' the storm and the night and the hell that surrounds her
I can see with a faith which immortals have given,
Burning words, blazing out o'er the portals of heaven,
"SHE WILL LIVE!"

But a part of the *freight* that our forefathers gave her,
We must cast to the deep yawning waters to save her,—

'Tis the chain for the slave we must fling out to light her,
'Tis the brand and the whip we must yield up to right her.
She will live.

Clean the decks of the curse—if opposed by the owner,
Hurl the wretch to the wave, as they hurled over Jonah,
With a "freedom to all," gleaming forth from our banner,
Let the tyrant yet learn we have *freemen* to man her,
She will live.

She will live while a billow lies swelling before her,
She will live while the blue arch of heaven bends o'er her;
While the name of a Christ to the fallen we cherish,
Till the hopes in the breast of humanity perish,
She will live.

THE TEMPLARS.

Dedicated to the members of St. John's Encampment, Bangor, Maine.

Who aid the widows with their mites,
And guard the helpless virgin's rights?—
A band of old and valiant Knights,
The Templars.

To save a friend, who walk around
With blood-stained feet, on frozen ground?

If any such are ever found—
They're Templars.

Who shield the Christians as they kneel,
And wall them in with burnished steel,
And guard them well thro' woe and weal?
The Templars.

What men are those, despite of scars,
Who, facing flashing scimetars,
Defend the Cross in Holy Wars?
The Templars.

When Knights are called from "labor" here,
Who throng around the sable bier,
And drop the warm, fraternal tear?—
The Templars.

God of our Craft, enable me
A faithful, worthy Knight to be,
And bring me home, at last, to Thee
A Templar.

TO JOHN BROWN IN PRISON.

Stand firm, John Brown, till your fate is o'er,
For the world, with an anxious eye,
Looks on as it seldom has looked before,
While the hour of your doom draws nigh—
Stand firm,
John Brown,
Stand firm!

Dread not the blow that a coward deals,
And fear not the tyrant's nod,
Doubt not the end of the work you would shape,
For you're shaping the work of God—
Stand firm,
John Brown,
Stand firm!

The outer John Brown they may torture and kill,
And tumble it into a grave,
But the inner John Brown will trouble them still,
By its whisperings 'round with the slave—
Stand firm,
John Brown,
Stand firm!

Death nears you, John Brown, old outer John Brown,
And marks you as food for the worm,
But death nor the worm can harm inner John Brown,
So inner John Brown, stand firm—
Stand firm,
John Brown,
Stand firm!
Old *inner* John Brown, Stand firm!

FANNIE WARD.

Full oft I have dreamed of the hours, Fannie Ward,
Full oft of those joy-laden hours,
We strolled from your cot, when your cheek was in bloom,
And sung with the birds in the bowers.

And well I remember the day, Fannie Ward—
That cheerless and sorrowful day—
My spirit was fainting and bleeding within,
When bearing you, lifeless, away.

This world has been dreary since then, Fannie Ward—
Most gloomy and dreary since then—
And sad were each moment, except for the hope
To meet you, in heaven, again.

Do you ever look down from the skies, Fannie Ward,
From your own happy home in the skies,

To note the wild throbs of my sorrowing heart,
  And count the tear-drops in my eyes?

Oh, grant me but this, only this, Fannie Ward,
  Oh, grant me, my lost one, but this:
Restrain me when tempted to swerve from the path
  Which leads to your haven of bliss.

That vow which I breathed as you died, Fannie Ward—
  That vow, in your ear, as you died—
Is fresh on my heart, as when kneeling, I pledged
  To make none but Fannie my bride.

ALL AT HOME.

Drive every care and pain the farthest distance,
  For we, the children ten,
And they, the two, who blest us with existence,
  Are all at home again.

Say not that three are dead and gone forever,
  Talk not to me of gloom,
Tell not of Jordan's cold and cheerless river,
  And brood not o'er the tomb.

We all are here, and God has not bereft us,
  Then every grief assuage;
They have not gone far off, but only left us,
  Like actors on the stage,

And stepped aside behind a sable curtain,
  Which briefly drops between;
The nine and three are busied dressing
  Just for another scene.

I hear their footfalls tinkling all around us,
  I see their shadowy forms now flitting by,
I feel the pressure of the tie that bound us,
  I breathe their teachings of philosophy.

Then drive each care and pain the farthest distance,
  For we, the children ten,
And they, the two, who blest us with existence,
  Are all at home again.

WHEN YOU AND I WERE BOYS.

To Gen. James Henry Carleton, U. S. A.

I'm dreaming of the days, dear James,
  Such days we ne'er shall know,
When happiness lived up this way,

Some twenty years ago:
When feet could stroll and hearts could beat,
And never feel fatigue,
Those times we swam, and fished, and sailed
Upon old Kenduskeag.

That stream now ripples just the same,
So calm, and clear, but still,
And turns that same old water-wheel,
Beneath that same old mill.
But now, dear James, that ancient mill
Another crew employs,
The crew now sleeps that run that mill,
When you and I were boys.

Where are those lads with whom we spelt
Within that school-house room.?
Some far away are hoarding gold,
Some rest within the tomb.
The change that time has written here,
Oft makes the tear-drop start,
And sends a sickening coldness through
Each fibre of my heart.

We've clambered up the hill of life—
How short the journey seems;

And now are pitching o'er the top,
  Bound to the land of dreams.
But when at last we reach the foot,
  And leave our earthly toys,
Oh, may we meet just as we met
  When you and I were boys.

n toddling down the dreary slope,
  Beset with dangerous snares,
Our locks bleached out by frosty winds,
  Our backs bent down by cares;
Full oft we'll stop to take a breath,
  And scare away fatigue,
By dreaming of our boyish sports
  Upon old Kenduskeag.

In battling through our pilgrimage,
  Amid the ceaseless strife,
And jostlings at each step we take,
  Throughout this warring life,
Oh, would it not exceed all bliss,
  Transcend all earthly joys,
To feel the freshness that we felt
  When you and I were boys.

ONE WORLD AT A TIME.

I doubt not that God has created some sphere,
  Some region of exquisite bliss,
More glorious, by far, than we journey thro' here,
  And free from the sorrows of this.

But mortals are dreaming, while plodding along,
  Too much of that heavenly clime ;
They'd better be singing this practical song—
  This motto: One world at a time.

To God, to yourself, to your fellow be just,
  To the winds toss your creeds and your sects,
And, leaving this world, with a confidence trust
  To the chances that follow the next.

YOU THOUSAND OF MEN.

Addressed to the 18th Maine Regiment on its departure for the seat of war, 1862.

Say, where are you going, you thousand of men?
      Now one thing is certain,
    That never, ah never
    This side the deep river,
      This side the dark curtain
    Just flung out to screen us,

Which drops down between us
And those who've passed over
That cold, stormy river,
No, never again
Shall this crowd ever meet you,
Shall this throng ever greet you,
In a bodily form,
With your hearts beating warm—
You thousand of men!

But, thank the Great Giver,
Though crossing that river,
Your barks may be shattered,
Your Outer Garbs tattered—
Thank God that again
From the mount you inherit,
You may come back in spirit,
All you who pass over
That cold, stormy river—
You may come back to meet us,
You may come back to greet us,
With your hearts beating warm,
In a blesseder form—
You thousand of men!

With the clearest of vision
I have witnessed the yearning

Of the troops now returning
From the land so elysian;
Of the troops who passed over
That cold, stormy river,
'Mid the roar and the rattle
Of a nation in battle—
So, quickly again,
From the mount you inherit,
You must come back to meet us,
You must come back to greet us,
You must come back in spirit,
With your hearts beating warm,
In a blissfuller form,
All you who pass over
That cold, stormy river—
From you thousand of men!

ACT YOURSELF.

If you ever act at all,
Act yourself;
Never try to ape another,
Sink or swim, or rise or fall,
Never imitate, but rather
Act yourself.

Brains than many have you less,
Act yourself,
Each for something must be fit,
Give me native foolishness,
Rather than this borrowed wit,—
Act yourself.

Elephants should never dance,
Act yourself:
Turkeys should not try to hound,
Women should not wear the pants,
Men should never wear the gown—
Act yourself.

Forms nor fashions never heed,
Act yourself;
Talk of *fashions* for a *man!*
Copies never *did* succeed,
And *mere* copies never can.—
Act yourself.

Human nature wants her way,
Act yourself.
Out upon the tricks of art,
When you have a word to say,
When you take the simplest part,
Act yourself.

A FEW WORDS

FROM MAINE TO MASSACHUSETTS ABOUT THE BURNS CASE.

"Massachusetts, God forgive her,
She's a kneeling 'mong the rest,
She that ought to have clung forever
In her grand old eagle-nest."

Is water running in your veins ?"
Have ye no pluck at all ;
What, stand and see a gyve put on
In sight of Faneuil Hall.

For many a long and tedious year
We've heard your people tell
About a little rise of land,
Where Joseph Warren fell.

Oh, brag no more about that spot,
Let every tongue be still,
But scratch the name of *Bunker* out,
And call it "Buncombe" Hill.

We have no Boston down in Maine,
No Massachusetts Bay,

No Plymouth Rock to tell the world,
  Where once the Mayflower lay,

No Garrisons, no Phillipses,
  No poets, martyrs, sages,
No mighty man to light a torch
  To lighten future ages.

And yet, with all our ignorance,
  We've often felt of late,
That Burns could never have been dragged
  From out the "Pine Tree State."

"THE FOOLS AIN'T ALL DEAD."

"The fools ain't all dead" is a maxim that's sounded
  From grog-shop and stable, from tavern and shed,
And truthfuller adage was never propounded,
  Than this modern proverb, "the fools ain't all dead."

While Virtue, in tatters, is shunned and neglected,
  And wanders an outcast, forlorn and distressed,
While Vice, in its tinsel, is wooed and respected—
  Invited and flattered, esteemed and caressed.

While Quackery the practice of Science is aping—
  Though Science goes hungry, while Quackery is fed—
While hundreds and thousands are greedily gaping
  To swallow a humbug, "the fools ain't all dead."

While kinsman with kinsman, or neighbor with neighbor,
  For merest of trifles will madly dispute,
And squander the proceeds of twenty years' labor
  To settle the quarrel by reference or suit;

While printers depend for their bread upon patrons;
  While ballots are sold for a demagogue's bow;
While damsels, despite of advice from the matrons,
  Will barter their all for a libertine's vow;

While striplings imagine that leaving the tillage,
  Where Nature designed them as fixtures for life,
And flocking, imported, to city or village,
  Imbued with the notions of Potiphar's wife;

That they, by a system of swelling and blowing,
  And long ere the hay-chaff has worked from the head,
Can fix the impression they're fellows worth knowing,
  'Tis fair to presume that "the fools ain't all dead."

While churchmen will argue that every true preacher
  Should pound out his sermon, by stamping and blows;

That learning disqualifies man for a teacher,
And gospel's not pure till it twangs through the nose;

While women conjecture that novels, before them,
Will stamp them forever as ladies of taste,
That man cannot fail to admire and adore them,
For smallness of feet and for hornet-like waist;

While fops are esteemed for the starch in the collar,
And bear's oil 's preferred to the brains in the head;
While merit's outweighed by the "almighty dollar,"
'Tis plain to be seen that "the fools ain't all dead."

"The fools ain't all dead," and my readers will know it,
For he who can hope to win glory or bread,
By leaving his law-books and turning to poet,
Illustrates the fact that "the fools ain't all dead."

THE LION AND THE SKUNK.

A DREAM.

I met a lion in my path,
('Twas on a dreary autumn night),
Who gave me the alternative
To either run or fight.

I dare not turn upon the track,
I dare not think to run away,

For fear the lion at my back,
  Would seize me as his prey.

So summoning a fearless air,
  Though all my soul was full of fight,
I said unto the forest king,
  I will not *run* but *fight.*

We fought, and as the fates decreed,
  I conquered in the bloody fray,
For soon the lion at my feet
  A lifeless carcase lay.

A little skunk was standing by,
  And noted what the lion spoke,
And when he saw the lion die,
  The lion's tracks he took.

He used the lion's very speech,
  For, stretching to his utmost height,
He gave me the alternative,
  To either run or fight.

I saw he was prepared to fling
  Fresh odors from his bushy tail,
And knew those odors very soon
  My nostrils would assail.

So summoning a humble air,
  Though all my soul was free from fright,
I said unto the dirty skunk:
  I'll *run* but will not *fight.*

MORAL.

As years begin to cool my blood,
  I rather all would doubt my spunk,
Than for a moment undertake
  To fight a human skunk.

OLD RUFUS RAY,

OR "WHEN THE PLACE WAS NEW."

In an ancient cottage yonder,
  Lives old Rufus Ray,
To that cottage oft I wander
  At the close of day.

Like a fixture now he lingers,
  On his bed of pain,
Grief has filched with thievish fingers,
  Reason from his brain.

Passing brief the words he utters,
  Senseless words, but few,

This, and only this he mutters:
  "When the place was new."

Years agone he loved a maiden,
  Blindly, fondly, true,
But she died with sorrow laden,
  "When the place was new."

Grief then filched with thievish fingers
  Reason from his brain;
Ever since this being lingers
  On his bed of pain.

God restore that long-lost maiden,
  Wretched man, to you,
May you meet at last in Aiden,
  Where "the place is new."

In a lonely cottage yonder,
  Breathes one Rufus Ray,
To that cottage let us wander,
  At the close of day.

We shall find he ever utters
  Senseless words, but few;
This, and only this he mutters:
  "When the place was new."

SAXON PLUCK.

Oh that some power would make and sell
  A different ink and pen,
That I might truly write and tell
  About one kind of men.

A set that's always sure to pass,
  And worlds can't wag without 'em—
A "yes-sir," "no-sir," dodging class,
  With no back-bone about 'em.

A scraping, bowing kind of folks,
  Who o'er the rounds are going,
And always watching weather-cocks,
  To see how winds are blowing.

If you hate colored gentlemen,
  And think yourselves above 'em
'Tis just as well to say so, then,
  As 'tis to say you love 'em.

Or think that slavery is worse
  Than any other evil;
A filching, eating, mildew curse,
  Begotten by the devil;

Then loose your tongues and talk it out,
  And let the Hunkers howl,—
No man is fit to be about
  Who trembles at a growl.

Or, if you say and truly think
  A statute touching toddy,
Is worse than certain pauper drink,
  Which kills the soul and body,

Repeal the law, or raise a storm,
  And pass around the "Cag,"
But do not shield your brandy form
  Behind a temperance flag.

But if you take the other tack,
  And say the law should stand,
And if you know it sluices back
  Damnation from the land,

Sustain the act in spite of knocks,
  And keep away the sin,
Though you must wade to ballot-box
  In purple to the chin.

But if you haven't get the nerve,
  An honest hand to show,

If you *will* quiver, nod and swerve,
Like saplings in a blow;

Your hobbies fix, and stand between,
And buckle if you must,
But mind it, men, 'tis shocking mean
To be a lapping dust.

For better far it is to say,
We will not curve the back,
Though pestilence shall hedge our way,
And sword be on our track.

I saw a temperance talker once,
Embrace a stupid bloat,
And dicker with the loathsome dunce,
For what?—to get his vote!

Methought I'd sooner bend my knees
To idols in the east
Than trim my sails to catch the breeze
Which blew from such a beast.

A spotless life is not my toast,
I never had the luck
Of being pure—then let me boast
Of good old SAXON PLUCK.

"OLD WILLEY."

Who cares in this crowd what a Homer says
  Of the warring men in the ancient days;
What matters it now to you or me
  Though the Iliad or Odyssey,
May tell of the the time when a Trojan corse
  Was tramped by the feet of a Grecian horse;
Though the epic song of the bard may state
  How Achilles fell at the Scaean Gate?
But it startles a world that I am come down
  To tell of a man from my native town:
Of a man, unknown, obscure and plain,
  But who once belonged to the 11th of Maine!

When Slavery, pressed by Freedom hard
  Fired up the heart of a Beauregard,
And the first red shot from Sumter fell
  And the Eagle screamed like a scream from hell;
When her shriek went out o'er vale and crag.
  As she clung like death to the dear old Flag,
And the first kind look she got, was one
  From a man named Robert Anderson,
I felt somehow, and I wrote and said
  That we had a big old trouble ahead.

With all my faith in God and such,
With all my religion, and that wan't much,
My faith wan't clear, and my hope wan't light
Till Daniel E. Willey went into the fight.

They called him "*Old Willey*," up there, I'm sure
'Tis a term oft used when our clothes get poor—
He laid the wall, and he sawed the wood
For me and others in the neighborhood;
He never could lecture and never could speak
One word of grammar, and couldn't read Greek,
Though he dwelt in that old school, 'tis true,
Where the old road butts at the avenue.
Through his leaky boots you could see his feet,
As he toiled for his daily food to eat;
For many a palm can never hold
The sordid dust that is scraped from gold.
Though he felled the trees and he tilled the lands
With his brawny arms and his horny hands,
It never entered a soldier's brain
That Willey would ever fight or train;
And never getting a draft or call
He sawed the wood and he laid the wall.

One day to my village two men rode down—
Yes, both came over from Stetson town,

And one was General Hill, I believe,
  He hadn't on then that empty sleeve;
I could told them quick that he wouldn't yield
  For a one right arm on the Deep Run field;
And the other fellow with Hill, they say
  Was General Plaisted, who talks to-day.
This Willey and I were standing o'er
  (He sawing wood) near my office door.
As the men from Stetson town rode by
  A neighbor of mine was standing nigh,—
With his traitor lips to the startled air
  He hissed the flag that was floating there.
Like a granite post Old Willey stood
  And his old saw dropped from the half-sawed wood;
Then he hoisted the strap round his big broad hips
  And he crumbled the pipe 'neath his firm blue lips;
And his burnt, tanned face gave a fiendish smile,
  But never a word did he speak the while
Till he glowered at the man hard by, and when
  He taunted that Union flag again,
Then his tortured nerves like a serpent coiled
  And these tough words from the old man boiled:
Says he "*Did you hear how that devil hissed;*
  By Jesus, Squire, I'm going to enlist!"
Though he split huge logs, he couldn't stand

The thought of a rift in his native land,
And he *did* enlist, for the brave old soul,
With his name on the gallant Plaisted's roll,
For the cast of a die, for a loss or gain,
With the gory, famed old 11th of Maine,
For a mortal fray with his kith and kind
Left a dying wife and a child behind,
Marched out to the front where he fought and bled,
And he came back maimed, and now he is dead.
With his folded arms he lies so still
In a cold, sound sleep on the "Crowell Hill."
I wish I knew if he felt the least
As he felt when our Father's flag was hissed;
For he slumbers there 'neath a beetling crag
By the side of the one who hissed the flag.

As we go all pale, with the boatman, o'er
In our final voyage to the other shore,
Mid the fearful surge of the rolling tide,
Sometimes you know,
That friend and foe
Will crouch and cuddle down side by side.

In the last review, somewhere beyond,
Of the world's grand army train;
When the books are read to an anxious throng

And they call for the 11th of Maine,
And the Judges come to Willey's case,
Looking so wise and grim;
Unless by some strange farce they rout,
And crush this life's remembrance out,
Or blot those scenes of warring strife
When battling for a Nation's life,
And from my soul wipe every trace
Of love for Country, Home and Race;
If any part of *me* is there,
In the face of every power I swear
If Willey finds no credit given,
Behind those balance sheets in Heaven,
For fighting in the 11th of Maine,
And reaps thereby no single gain—
Although a spirit death I die
With loss of immortality,
Should I find his case is going hard
I'll help the old man "run the guard"
Ere the gold gate swings on him.

HOPE OF BLISS.

SIXTEEN LINES.

Build barriers high, and wide and deep,
To wall your castes apart,
Such fortresses can never keep
The heart from answering heart.

A magic, telegraphic cord
Extends from soul to soul,
On which leap burning thought and word,
Despite of man's control.

The king, with crown upon his head,
The beggar at his gate,
The Christian on his dying bed,
The convict at his grate,

One common hope together share,
A boon for rich and poor,
Each to that hope a rightful heir,
A hope of bliss in store.

MY LAST REQUEST.

Brethren of our mystic order,
  Bound together by a tie,
Olden, sacred and enduring,
  Come and see a Craftsman die.

Watch like angels round my pillow,
  Till the ransomed spirit flies
To its Excellent Grand Master,
  In his lodge above the skies.

Oft we've met upon the Level,
  Let us part upon the Square—
Perfect Ashlers in the temple,
  May we meet together there.

Let no stranger's hand entomb me
  Underneath the tufted sod,
None except a brother Mason
  Should consign my dust to God.

Heave no formal sigh of sorrow
  O'er the ashes of the dead,
Only plant the priceless symbol,
  Freshly blooming at my head.

When death's gavel sound shall call you
  Off from Labor unto rest,
May you, Craftsmen, find Refreshment
  In the mansions of the blest.

NEVER GET READY TO DIE.

Up, up, and give fight to the legions of wrong,
  Give zealots and bigots the lie,
Who cantingly tell you, with faces so long,
  That all should get ready to die.

This world is too full of your dying ones, now,
  And we need in this terrible strife,
Not souls that are pining and fainting, I trow,
  But souls that have vigor and life.

While one lift at humanity's wheels you can give,
  Or one tear you can wipe from the eye,
Get ready, my brother, *keep* ready to *live*,
  But never get ready to die.

WHEN, WHERE, AND HOW SHALL I DIE.

When shall I die?

It may be, perchance, to-morrow,
Ere a larger, newer sorrow
Comes around my soul to borrow
Half the bliss it saves;
It may be when locks are bleaching,
When life's lengthened shadow's teaching
That my feet are swiftly reaching
Near a place for graves.

Where shall I die?

It may be with tearless stranger,
It may be mid toil and danger,
It may be in hut or manger,
Far from friends removed;
It may be when friends are near me,
Breathing kindly words to cheer me—
Few, who neither scorn nor fear me,
Friends my heart has proved.

How shall I die?

It may be when doubts assail me,
When my trust in God shall fail me,

While a horde of phantoms hail me
  From a land of gloom;
It may be when hope attends me,
When a world's Redeemer sends me
Living, dying faith, that lends me
  Peace beyond the tomb.

Thou Great Architect of Power,
Though my sky of life must lower,
Aid me in death's awful hour,
  Save me from despair—
When I cross the stormy river,
Be my bark, my pilot, ever,
Leave me, God of mercy, never,—
  This is all my prayer.

THE SOLDIERS OF MEDUXNEKEAG.

Come on with me now, let us travel on,
  Not far, not many a league,
From the spot where the old and the bold St. John
  Locks hands with Meduxnekeag.

As a pay or a fee, for this stroll with me,
  I will tell you a tale to-day,
Of the wife, the mother, the widow—all three—
  And the soldiers—Robert Gray.

It was here, very near where we stroll to-day,
  Where the grim old barrack stands,
That a girl, in the pride of her youth, they say
  With a Sergeant Gray locked hands.

But death stole into those barrack walls,
  Which stood near the river's banks,
And entered the name of that Sergeant Gray
  On the list of his spectre ranks.

But the years rolled by at Meduxnekeag,
  When quick came a country's call
For the name of her own—of her manly boy—
  Through a rent in that barrack wall.

She bade him go forth from Meduxnekeag,
  To his God and his country true—
She bade him go forth, this young Robert Gray,
  Clad out in his Union blue.

He went, but he wandered not back again
  To the roof near the river's banks—
He went like his father, old Sergeant Gray,
  To fill up death's spectre ranks.

From the charge on that field, that was steeping in gore,
He went where the brave spirits dwell,
With "no matter for me, but push on my brave boys,"
Ringing out o'er the shot and the shell.

What is that crouching there, in the barrack nook,
Bowed down by the hand of dismay?
There's a trace in her face of the laughing girl—
'Tis the mother of Robert Gray!

Let us leave these weird walls at Meduxnekeag,
I'm too old and ashamed to cry,
And I feel that the tears are rushing fast
For the crow's feet 'round my eye.

But my friends, if you worship a God in this life,
And you ever kneel down to pray,
Remember the mother—the widow—the wife
Of the soldiers—Robert Gray.

GIVE THEM BREAD AND NOT A STONE.

[At a meeting of the Grand Lodge of Maine in 1851, a resolution was introduced authorizing the appropriation of a certain amount of the Lodge Funds for the purchase of a block for the Washington monument. The Hon. Comp. Ezra B. French, of Damariscotta, opposed the passage of the resolution in a very eloquent speech. In the course of his remarks he said: "*When the orphan children of our dead brethren throng around us destitute and tearful and ask for bread, will ye give them a stone?*"]

First dry that orphan's tears,
  And hush that orphan's cries,
Then pile up, if ye will,
  Your marble to the skies.

But, Craftsmen, spare that fund,
  Part earnings of the dead,
A pittance laid aside
  To buy their orphans bread.

Touch not a single dime,
  But let that fund alone—
'Tis mocking God and man,
  To barter it for stone.

'Tis better, better far,
  No monument should rise,
To tell the hallowed spot
  Where any hero lies,

Than that one orphan child
  Should pine for want of bread,
Or gold be squandered off,
  By which that child is fed.

First dry that orphan's tears,
  And hush that orphan's cries,
Then pile up, if ye will,
  Your marble to the skies.

MAKE YOUR MARK.

In the quarries should you toil,
                Make your mark,
Do you delve upon the soil,
                Make your mark,
In whatever path you go,
  In whatever place you stand,
Moving swift or moving slow,
  With a firm and honest hand,
                Make your mark.

Should opponents hedge your way,
                Make your mark,
Work by night, or work by day,
                Make your mark,

Struggle manfully and well,
  Let no obstacles oppose,
None right-shielded ever fell
  By the weapons of his foes,
          Make your mark.

What though born a peasant's son,
          Make your mark,
Good by poor men can be done,
          Make your mark,
Peasant's garbs may warm the cold,
  Peasant's words may calm a fear,
Better far than hording gold
  Is the drying of a tear,
          Make your mark.

Life is fleeting as a shade,
          Make your mark,
Marks of some kind must be made,
          Make your mark,
Make it while the arm is strong,
  In the golden hours of youth,
Never, never make it wrong,
  Make it with the stamp of truth
          Make your mark.

"PIOUS LIKE HELL."

A few years since a powerful revival of religion was witnessed at Oldtown, Maine. Among the hopeful converts was an Indian of the Penobscot tribe, who, soon after his conversion, attended a prayer-meeting, and was called upon to "tell his experience." Not exactly understanding the construction of the King's English, Peol expressed himself as follows: "Oh, glory; me feel pious like hell." That incident suggests the following stanzas:

The hand of religion is potent to save,
   Its value no mortal can prize,
It leads us in safety clear down to the grave,
   Then gives us a pass to the skies.
But since the grand choice in the garden was given,
   Since Adam from Paradise fell,
Full many are found to be pious like heaven,
   While many are "pious, like hell."

I once was an orphan boy, mortgaged and leased,
   And served without hope of a fee,
For one who was lending the Lord what she fleeced
   From the girl in the kitchen and me.
'Twas a day or two since that I gazed on the face
   Of her, the once mademoiselle,
And thought—tho' she bragged of "abounding in grace"—
   Of Peol, and "pious like hell."

But tares in the wheat, nor the counterfeit coin,
  Should rob us no night of our rest,—
Let this be our motto while journeying on:
  God orders all things for the best.
And mind it, no knowledge to mortals is given,
  By which that frail mortal can tell,
Except by the fruits, who is pious like heaven,
  Or, Peol-like, "pious, like hell."

THE MASON'S DEATH AND BURIAL.

The old church bell struck a startling note,
  And sent forth a solemn knelling,
While every peal from his brazen throat
  Of a sundered tie was telling.

And soon I heard from a Craftsman, woe,
  And the summons hastily spoken,
That a brother was passed from the lodge below,
  That a link in our chain was broken.

With a quivering lip and a glistening tear,
  Each Craftsman speedily hurried
To see that the cold, pale sleeper there,
  In an ancient form was buried.

We laid him down in his lonely tomb,
  Our hearts o'ercharged with sorrow,
But saw through the mystic sprig in bloom
  The gleam of a brighter morrow.

The sickening sound of the falling sod,
  Which covered our brother's coffin,
Was lost in the wails that rose to God
  From the widowed wife and orphan.

Ah, little they dreamed in that darksome hour,
  When the bitter tears were gushing,
And fell despair, with a tyrant's power,
  The stricken heart was crushing,

Of a pledge we breathed to our brother at rest,
  Who lies in his narrow coffin,
A balm that shall soothe the troubled breast
  Of that widowed wife and orphan.

JOHN WARNER'S NOT DEAD.*

Why mourn you—the Craft? for John Warner's not dead,
  Though his body lies pulseless and still,
That missile which forced its fierce way through the head,
  No *real* John Warner could kill.

John Warner's not dead, though the casket is dumb,
  But has gone on a mission of love,
With his Compass and Square, with his Level and Plumb,
  To his work in the Grand Lodge above.

John Warner's not dead, but will often return,
  And oft in *our* Lodge will appear,
And o'er his cold ashes which lie in the urn,
  Will whisper the Word in our ear.

John Warner's not dead—by each hope in my breast,
  I would swear on this spot where I stand,
That since the last sun sank in silence to rest,
  I have felt the Strong Grip from his hand.

* John Warner, of Kenduskeag, a member of Pacific Lodge, Exeter, Me., No. 64, and of the 2d Maine Regiment, was accidentally shot in camp, at Hall's Hill, Va., Feb. 24, 1862, and was buried with Masonic honors at Kenduskeag, March 7, 1862.

INFLUENCE AND RETRIBUTION.

Ye cannot send the simplest line
  Abroad from off your pen,
But ye must meet, in future hour,
  That very line again.

The slightest word ye cannot speak
  Within a mortal ear,
But that the echo of such word
  Ye must forever hear.

Ye cannot stride one single step,
  While journeying here below,
But that some brother takes your path
  For happiness or woe.

Unholy thoughts ye cannot think,
  Though never once expressed,
But that some demon plucks those thoughts,
  To fill another's breast.

Then watch your pen with miser care,
  And let its labors be
A fount of solace to the soul,
  And not of misery.

And guard your lips, nor let them speak
 A word, which future years
Can by some magic process change
 To bitter, burning tears.

And mark the road on which you stand,
 And note your footsteps well,
And shun that broad, frequented track,
 Which leads away to hell.

And check your vain, unholy thoughts,
 As much as in you lies,
Nor let them rob you of that bliss
 Beyond the starry skies.

TRY AGAIN.

Should your cherished purpose fail,
 Try again,
Never falter, never quail,
 Try again.
Nerve the arm and raise the hand,
 Fling the outer garments by,
With a dauntless courage stand,
 Shouting forth the battle-cry,
 Try again.

Is your spirit bowed by grief,
Try again,
Rally quick, for life is brief,
Try again;
Every saint in yonder sphere,
Borne through tribulation there,
Whispers in the anxious ear
Of each mortal, in despair,
Try again.

What though stricken to the earth,
Try again—
Up, as from a second birth,
Try again.
Yonder flower beneath the tread,
Struggling when the foot has gone,
Rising feebly in its bed,
Tells the hopeless looker-on
Try again.

Guided by the hand of Right,
Try again,
With Hope's taper for a light,
Try again,
With a destiny like ours,

And that destiny to choose,
With such God-created powers,
And a heaven to gain or lose,
Try again.

APOSTROPHE TO A GONG.

They say, old thunderer, that away in China,
Some thousand miles the other side of earth,
Where tea is grown beyond the ocean briny,
Near the big, ancient wall, thou hadst thy birth.
If true or not, the one who gave thee breath,
Ought to have lived until he starved to death.

No doubt that China-man once kept an inn,
And was a Shylock and a hardened sinner,
Who, for the sole and naked thirst for "*tin*,"
Conspired to cheat his guests of half a dinner;
And so the old, penurious, wicked sprite
Invented thee, to kill the appetite.

Strange that the love of gold and power of error
Should propagate upon the human brain,
And proffer birth to such a child of terror—
A progeny to fill the world with pain,

An instrument of woe, that only serves
To furnish torture for the feeble nerves.

I fear there is a hell—our Bibles teach it—
And reason, conscience, say the Bible's true,
And lettered priests in every nation preach it,
Except a modern, theoretic few
Insurance agents, peddling out for hire
Sham policies against eternal fire.

But in those dark and foul and burning regions,
Whose direful noises echo loud and long,
There is no sound sent forth by hellish legions
One-half so horrid as thy noise, oh Gong.
For wild and fearful though their howlings be,
They are, to thine, a perfect symphony!

THE EMPTY SLEEVE.

By the moon's pale light, to this gazing throng,
Let me tell one tale, let me sing one song—
'Tis a tale devoid of an aim or plan,
'Tis a simple song of a one arm man;
Till this very hour, I could ne'er believe
What a tell-tale thing is an empty sleeve—
What a weird, queer thing is an empty sleeve.

It tells in a silent tone to all
Of a country's need and a country's call,
Of a kiss and a tear for a child and wife,
And a hurried march for a nation's life;
Till this very hour, would you e'er believe
What a tell-tale thing is an empty sleeve—
What a weird, queer thing is an empty sleeve.

It tells of a battle-field of gore,
Of the sabre's clash, of the cannon's roar,
Of the deadly charge—of the bugle's note,
Of a gurgling sound in a foeman's throat,
Of the whizzing grape—of the fiery shell,
Of a scene which mimics the scenes of hell;
Till this very hour, who could e'er believe
What a tell-tale thing is an empty sleeve—
What a weird, queer thing is an empty sleeve.

Though it points to a myriad wounds and scars,
Yet it tells that a flag, with the stripes and stars,
In God's own chosen time will take
Each place of the rag with the rattle-snake,
And it points to a time when that flag will wave
O'er a land where there breathes no cowering slave;
To the top of the skies let us all then heave
One proud hurrah for the empty sleeve!
For the one arm man, and the empty sleeve!

THE REBELLION.

There's a law of compensation and a law of retribution
For each mortal and each nation,
And I've seen the plain solution.
If there's truth in the evangel
Then the old recording angel,
By that law of compensation,
And that law of retribution,
For I've seen the whole solution,
Has a reckoning with this nation.

I have seen the primal entry
In the books beyond the sentry,
Of the sentry standing ever
Gaunt and grim beside the river;
At the bridge that passes over,
At the dark bridge with the cover.

On a midnight dark and dreary,
When my form was weak and weary,
Then my spirit left its dwelling,
Left it in another's keeping,
In the kind care of another,
Of a loving angel brother,

Who had left his earth friends weeping,
And had crossed the river swelling,
But had found a passage over
Through the dark bridge with the cover;
And had made another entry
On the shore this side the sentry,
Of the sentry standing ever
Gaunt and grim beside the river.

As my spirit made its entry
On the shore beyond the sentry,
Of the sentry standing ever
Gaunt and grim beside the river,
At the bridge that passes over,
At the dark bridge with the cover,
There I met the writing angel,
With his records all before him,
And a halo hanging o'er him,
With his books named in the evangel.
With a saddened, anxious feeling,
Through my inner spirit stealing,
Turned I to the writing angel,
With his books named in the evangel,
Just to learn the situation
Of our struggling, bleeding nation;

Just to learn this from the entry
On the books beyond the sentry,
Of the sentry standing ever
Gaunt and grim beside the river,
At the bridge that passes over,
At the dark bridge with the cover.

With a tear the angel said it,
"*There's your debt, and there's your credit.*
Just inspect each primal entry
On the books this side the sentry,
Of the sentry standing ever
Gaunt and grim beside the river,
At the bridge that passes over,
At the dark bridge with the cover."
Turned I quick aside the cover,
And I glanced the pages over,
And I found the primal entry
On the books beside the sentry,
Of the sentry standing ever,
Gaunt and grim beside the river,
At the bridge that passes over,
At the dark bridge with the cover,
Was before the old embargo,
When the Dutch ship with her cargo

Ploughed her keel across our waters,
With her fettered sons and daughters.
'Twas a charge for countless terrors,
And the middle passage horrors.
Turned I then again the cover,
And I searched the pages over,
But I found no credit entry
On the books beyond the sentry,
Of the sentry standing ever
Gaunt and grim beside the river,
At the bridge that passes over,
At the dark bridge with the cover.
Then I gave unto the angel
All his books named in the evangel,
When a deep and saddened feeling
Came across my spirit stealing;
But the angel sternly said it—
"*You shall have your honest credit.*"
Then the next and second entry
On the books beyond the sentry,
Of the sentry standing ever
Gaunt and grim beside the river,
Was the wails of wives and mothers,
And for fathers, sisters, brothers—

When the auction hammer thundered
That all human ties were sundered.

Then the next and final entry
On the books beyond the sentry,
Of the sentry standing ever
Gaunt and grim beside the river,
At the bridge that passes over,
At the dark bridge with the cover,
Was the proceeds of the cargo,
Brought before the old embargo;
And I found the angel had it,
With each mill of interest added.
But we pass now to the credit,
As the writing angel had it—
"When your land is filled with terrors,
Like the middle passage horrors,
All the horrors of each cargo,
Since the Dutch keel ploughed your waters,
With her sable sons and daughters,
Long before the slave embargo;
When your wails of wives and mothers,
Of your fathers, sisters, brothers,
Shall amount through all your slaughters,
To the wails of sons and daughters,

Of the sable sons and daughters,
Since the auction hammer thundered
That all human ties were sundered ;
When the proceeds of the cargo,
Brought before the old embargo,
When the proceeds as you had it,
With each mill of interest added,
Shall be squandered in your slaughters,
Mid your wails of wives and daughters,
You will get your honest credit."

Then he closed the opening cover,
When again I crossed the river,
By the sentry standing ever,
Gaunt and grim beside that river,
Then my spirit sought its dwelling,
Left within another's keeping,
Of an angel brother's keeping,
When my brother left this dwelling,
And re-crossed the river swelling
From the land with sorrow laden,
To his better home in Aidenn.

THE SPANKED BOTTOM.

Though years have fled, I mind it yet,
I and my lawyer brother,
Would badger, bother, tire and fret
A kind, old praying mother.

Her words would scarcely leave her there,
Ere he and I forgot 'em,
When, as a substitute for prayer,
She spanked our youthful bottom.

With inward threat, and outward pout,
I and my legal brother,
Agreed that heaven had dealt us out
A rash and cruel mother.

Since then, as on life's billows tossed,
With sin's old chains a clanking,
I find those teachings were not lost,
That praying and that spanking.

Mid smiles and tears—mid hopes and fears,
And creeds that long have bound me,
This is the last song of my years,
For each God's child around me:

We need some secret power aloft,
  To rule, direct and love us,
And need our spirit bottoms oft
  Spanked by some hand above us.

THE HAMMER AND THE ANVIL.

Improve your hour as best you may,
  Keep up your fitful clamor;
I chance to be the anvil, now,
  You chance to be the hammer.

Although to deal the heaviest stroke,
  Your heated nerves are straining,
The thinking, passive anvil gives
  No token of complaining.
Although the falling hammer, now,
  The dented face is scorning,
Your patient anvil, in its ring,
  Sends forth this note of warning—

Remember, 'mid your causeless blows,
  Remember, 'mid your clamor,
You yet may be the anvil, boys,
  And I may be the hammer.

WRITTEN FOR THE PROPOSED MEETING

OF NORTHERN AND SOUTHERN MASONS IN MASSACHUSETTS.

Craftsmen, craving kindly greeting,
Doff your blue and gray,
Let us hold one cordial meeting
On the Square, to-day.

Whether coming from our regions,
Where the pine-tree grows—
Whether coming from your legions,
Where the orange blows;

From plebeians, or from princes,
Owning gold or dross,
Sing we "*in hoc, signo vinces,*"
Marching 'round the Cross.

If war's thundering roar and rattle
Haunt our memories still,
Let them come from that old battle
Fought on Bunker's Hill;

Let each blackened corpse of passion,
 In its casements rot—
Plant no mystic sprig Acacian
 E'er to mark the spot.

Let us bury feuds, forever,
 Deep in common graves;
Let us quaff, for now or never,
 From Lethean waves.

When we cross the final ferry,
 Claiming earth no more—
When we step from out the wherry,
 On that distant shore,

We will strike one harp and tymbal
 At the master's calls;
We will use one word and symbol
 In the mystic halls.

A SONG FOR THE BOYS.

Stand up my boys, form in the ring,
Look sober and behave,
And if you want to hear one sing,
Just hear your uncle Dave.

But mind it, boys, I'll only try
To sing for you, who, hurled
And knocked about, have had to lie
Spoon-fashion to the world.

Whose peasant fathers gave you life,
Mixed in with toil and care,
And sent you forward to the strife
With hay-seed in your hair.

You red-haired urchin—stop that noise—
I'll not detain you long,
I never trouble men nor boys
With any tedious song.

This world, though some incline to call
It full of grips and grabs,
Is just the place, boys, after all
To learn your A B Abs.

And any man or boy will find,
  If not a hopeless fool,
That after all 'tis not behind
  A woman's summer school.

Whatever voyage in life you make,
  Though driven before the blast,
Leave something in the troubled wake,
  To show that you have passed.

Let ruin come, if come it must,
  But never act the knave,—
Be loyal, virtuous and just,
  Just like your Uncle Dave.

FIVE STANZAS.

Grasp your paddle, take your boat,
  Row the course you think is best,
But you shouldn't face the east
  While you paddle to the west,
                    Never.

Fight for virtue or for vice,
  On your passage to the grave;

Never sit astride the fence;
  Be an honest man or knave,
            Ever.

Go for error or for truth;
  Go for darkness or for light;
Paint your flag and hang it out,
  Be it black or be it white,
            Ever.

Have a notion of your own;
  Speak that notion plain and flat;
Be a mouse or be a bird;
  Never try to play the bat,
            Never.

Never ape the tad-pole, man;
  Never swim around incog;
Off with tail or off with claws;
  Be a polliwog or frog,
            Ever.

LINES ADDRESSED TO JOHN A. HILL,

CAPT. OF CO. K, 11TH ME. REG'T, AT A PUBLIC MEETING IN STETSON.

Welcome back again, brave soldier,
From your fields of fire and flood;
Welcome to your scenes of childhood,
Tho' your hands be stained with blood.

From the pallid lips of weakness;
From the florid lips of health;
From the poor man in his tatters;
From the rich man in his wealth;

From the old man, toddling to you,
Trusting to his faithful cane;
From the wee ones at the window,
Prattling through the broken pane;

From your brethren with the lambskin,
And their mystic grip and sign;
From the poet, in his frenzies,
Coming from the fabled nine;

There's a greeting for you, soldier,
From the great and from the small;
There's a welcome for you, Craftsman—
There's a welcome from us all.

THE POET'S INVITATION.

If I have found upon this mortal plain,
  One whose full heart to mine an echo gives;
Who notes my hope, my fear, my bliss, my pain,
  Come where a poet lives.
    Not to my walls, where justice blushes decked
      With legal quibbles and the foolish flaw,
    Where the best gushings of the soul are wrecked
      Among the mists of law;
Not to my curtained room, so primly cold,
  Filled with formalities so dull and drear,
Whose latticed bars, to chase away the mould,
  Are opened once a year;
    Not to my room, where the grim, miser chest
      Sends forth its creakings from its iron lid,
    To tell some heir, when life escapes my breast,
      Where ghostly gains are hid;
But come where my best treasures caper round
  Upon the worn, and on the dented floor;
Where blessed tiny hand-prints may be found
  Upon the cup-board door;
    Come to my home, where every trifle tells,
      In summing up the ills and joys of life,
    Not to the home where my dear *lady* dwells,
      But where I keep my *wife*.

THE BEVELLED GRIND-STONE.

Some thirty years ago, or so,
  When I lived with my mother,
I knew a man, whose name was Joe,
  And Simon, his half brother.

Now Simon was a whole-soul man,
  Though often getting mellow;
But Joe was made on a different plan—
  A most penurious fellow.

This Joe—for so the neighbors say—
  Told Simon, his half brother,
He thought it might be made to pay
  To run a grind-stone together.

They bought the stone, when Joe, you know,
  Just ground it to a bevel;
For, as I said before, this Joe
  Was meaner than the devil.

He gave the left side of the stone
  To Simon, his half brother,
And run the right-hand side alone,
  While Simon run the other.

When neighbors came to grind—now mind,
  And Joe—the mean one—finding
They had no coin to pay—they say
He gave them Simon's side to grind,
  Who charged no fee for grinding.

As time rolled on, they say, one day
  That Joe came in a frothing;
For, grinding on the other side,
Old Simon's bevel-side grew *wide*,
  While Joe's run off to *nothing*.

MORAL.

I sing to each earth-child around,
  To each whose "*head is level*":
When piled beneath that six-foot mound,
If not before, you'll surely find
'Tis just as well to let folks grind
  Upon your side the bevel.

THE WHEAT AND THE TARES.

Oh, 'tis many a year,
In the country, up here,
  Since the wheat and the tares
  Grew together in pairs—
Like a sister and brother,
Like a father and mother—
Without one or the other
  Always "putting on airs."

Then when the storm came,
  And the big thunder hurled
  Many a bolt at the world,

Then the wheat and the tares,
  Growing timid, appalled,
And, forgetting each name
  By which they were called,

And forgetting the threat
  As to which should be burned,
They each to the other
  Instinctively turned.

Yes, the wheat and the tares,
In the midst of their fight,
'Mid the gloom of the night,
Leaned on to each other—
Like a sister and brother,
Like a father and mother—
Without one or the other
Even "putting on airs."

THE SIX FELLOWS.*

'Twas yesterday—or day before—
I, and a country cousin,
Saw six grave fellows on a seat,
(Near half a "*baker's* dozen.")

'Twas latish in the afternoon,
And rather chilly weather—
So these six fellows, in a box,
Were huddled up together.

* Published in the Bangor Daily *Whig and Courier*, accompanied by the following remarks by the editor:—"The following impromptu lines were dashed off by their witty and gifted author during a few lounging minutes in the Court room, the other afternoon, where six judges were holding a Law term."

Now some of them would talk aloud,
And some of them would mutter—
And some of them were lank and lean,
And some were fat as butter.

Another fellow †—'cause the seat
Wán't wide enough to hold him—
Sat near, and with a pen wrote down
What these six fellows told him.

Two other fellows with the six
Make eight, when all together;
Perhaps these fellows staid away
Because 'twas rainy weather.

I noticed these six fellows there—
Who in a kind of line were—
Wore merely middling kind of clothes,
And not so good as mine were.

They sat and looked upon some books—
I think they call them dockets;
They had no blacking on their boots—
No watches in their pockets.

† Reporter of Decisions.

I gazed upon those fellows there,
  And as the twilight streamed off,
Strange fancies flittered thro' my brain,
  Few mortals ever dreamed of;

For, these six fellows hold a power—
  A power for good or evil—
Which, analyzed and understood,
  Would fright the very devil.

For soon these fellows separate,
  And scoot about to try us;
The place they go I most forget,
  But think 'tis "*Nisi Prius.*"

And if one fellow makes a bull,
  And we poor fellows feel it,
They have a right to meet again—
  And have the power to heal it.

The dog you love, the horse you drive,
  The gold mines you are selling,
The hut where shivering children sleep,
  The palace that you dwell in;

The loaf now steaming for a meal,
  The quill-wheel or your carriage;
The baby mewling in your lap,
  The wife you won at marriage;

That last memento, dear as breath,
  By some departed, given—
Love's golden chain, forged out by death,
  To link this life with heaven,

Some knavish whelp may up and claim
  Before the sun has risen—
And these six fellows, on that bench,
  Have power to say they're "hisen."

Grave, worthy seniors, just one word—
  You, on that seat together—
You, counting six, and with the two,
  Now tell me, frankly, whether

You deem, because you have the right
  To stop the bells from chiming,
And have the power to take one's breath,
  That you can stop my rhyming?

Sage men, a *private* word with you—
  You, on that seat together—
You, of the six, and with the two,
  Once more, now tell me, whether

With all your Courtly wisdom here,
  And all your power for terrors,
There may not be some higher Power—
  Some upper "Court of Errors?"

BILLY DEE.

Come, dwellers in this mortal tent,
  Just step aside and see
The cold and fleshly tenement,
  Where dwelt poor Billy Dee.

When Billy's house grew old and poor,
  From life's rude storms and wind,
He battered down the outer door,
  And left the wreck behind.

But in that land where Billy went,
  Each kind and generous brother
Gave something from his spirit tent
  To build him up another.

A WELCOME

TO THE HUGH DE PAYEN COMMANDERY OF KNIGHTS TEMPLAR, MELROSE, MASSACHUSETTS, AT BANGOR, JULY 20, 1869.

Craftsmen, listen to my sayings:—
Welcome, welcome, Hugh De Payens,
From old Massachusetts Bay,
To our climes where Boreas bloweth,
Where the sturdy pine-tree groweth,
Welcome to our shores to-day.

From your land, with age so hoary,
Land of pilgrim, song and story,
From your living streets and marts,
From your sacred soil of Warren,
Welcome to our cliffs, though barren,
Welcome to our homes and hearts.

Welcome as the old Crusader,
From the Palestine invader
Bringing back the sabre scar,
Mid the songs and feasts and dances,
And the flash of virgin glances,
Making sweet the fruits of war.

Gallant members of our order
Who have crossed the Cyprian border,
Join us in a song to-day,

With a curse (and not a lament)
For a Philip and a Clement,
And a tear for De Molay.

Banish now each cankering sorrow,
Banish each fear of to-morrow,
While we gather round our feast;
While the thought of rank we smother,
Welcome here each "Serving Brother,"
Welcome "Knight" and welcome "Priest." *

Welcome here each sworn defender
Of the helpless virgin tender,
And the ancient Calvary cross;
Bear it, like our Great Exemplar,
Bear it, patiently, each Templar,
Though the end be gain or loss.

When the full earth path we travel,
And the click of Death's dark gavel
Falls upon the leaden ear,
May we meet the Prince of princes
Shouting "*in hoc signo vinces*,"
In some new, celestial sphere.

* Three classes of the "Order of the Temple" in the 12th Century, viz:—"Serving Brothers," "Knights" and "Priests."

FAITH, HOPE, CHARITY.

Distrust not every form without—
  Than live through life such living death—
In the betraying fiend of Doubt,
  Have Faith.

Though through a blindman's-buff we're led,
  Or though in dusky paths we grope,
In a blest *something*, just ahead,
  Have Hope.

The treacherous blocks we may not see,
  O'er which our stumbling brothers fall—
So then have God-like Charity
  For all.

With these—the three—we may be blest,
  And leave behind us, when we go,
Around Life's sunset, in the west,
  A glow.

Then onward press, though for the grave,
  And calmly meet the closing strife—
Death is the only proof we have
  Of life.

LINES

SUGGESTED BY WENDELL PHILLIPS' LECTURE ON THE LOST ARTS.

You knew that brickyard where we used to play,
And the old Lombard horse that ground the clay;

From year to year that bobtail nag was found
Hitched to the sweep upon his clayey round;

And a new horse, you know, would only find
The marks and scenes the old nag left behind.

One day when straddle of that horse's back—
Proud as a conquering Roman on the track,

Filled to the lips with hominy and bliss—
I had this dream, which Phillips claims as his:

Man moves in circles—not in onward lines—
And every track and every truth he finds,

And every thought that makes him smile or weep,
Were left by others, pulling 'round the sweep.

PRAYERS AND KISSES.

This morn I saw a stern man kneel—
  One of the holy order—
He had a white robe round him wrapped,
  With black upon its border.

Just at my front a roguish boy
  Sat there, among the many,
With laughing eyes, whose name I learned,
  Was little Murray Dana.

And, at my left, a cherub girl
  Wore smiles as thick as spatter,
While little Murray, now and then,
  Was throwing kisses at her.

Pray on, stern man—God give you light—
  To you the task is given
To guide our stumbling feet aright
  And lead the way to heaven.

And you, my boy, keep at your task,
  Till death's cold chains have bound you,
With laughing eyes and merry heart,
  Throw kisses all around you.

For, mid the throng, that, at the last,
  The gate of glory misses,
Some may be found upon their knees
  As well as throwing kisses.

THOUGHTS AT A FUNERAL.

My memory holds one thing intact,
  That he, who lies so low,
Did me a generous, kindly act
  In the long years ago.

Since then, the teachings of the brain
  Or feelings of the heart,
Have held for each a different reign,
  And kept our paths apart.

But now amid death's awful night,
  With tapers burning dim,
I hold my screen to catch the light,
  And not the shades from him.

MARY DEE.

'Tis well that poor old Mary Dee,
Some little rest has found,
For she has washed full fifty years
For all the folks around.

Her soldier husband, "Billy Dee,"
I told you once, you know,
Was captured on Death's skirmish line,
Some sixty days ago.

In any hearing up above,
I shall be glad to tell
This much, or more, of Mary Dee:
She did her washings well—

That by her mild, unlettered tongue,
No fuss was ever made—
That when she got her washing through,
She smoked, or sung, or prayed.

If Mary and poor Billy meet
Beyond Death's sombre screen,
The first of Mary's care will be
That Billy's robe is clean.

THE BLIND GATEMAN.

I claim the legal right to boast,
For sure I felt a pride,
When I, with learn'd Judge Appleton
Close seated at my side,
To-day, around your city walls,
Was taking such a ride;—

Around your classic Lovers'-leap,
And famous old High head—
Around Mount Hope, where many a tear
Has crystalized the dead;
My steed, held firm, by bit and rein,
With willing foot step fled

Around full many a beetling crag,
So threatening and bold—
And many a weird and shattered home,
Reared in the days of old—
And many a towering, lordly roof
That hints of treasured gold.

At last that steed, with hurrying hoof,
Took Judge and poet o'er,
And halted with a conscious look

At Penury's cold door—
Those arid lands where city chiefs
Have garnered up their poor.

One thing I swear by every saint
Who dwells above the skies—
Believe me, now, the thing is true,
We found, to our surprise,
That he who swung the gate was blind,
Because he had no eyes!

They say for years that man has stood
Within that self-same place,
And swung that ponderous pauper gate
With the same measured pace,
And gazed with that strange, blinded stare
Into each passer's face.

I trust, that at the pearly gate,
The Judge and I shall find
The gateman there, who lets them in,
Like Paul Demeritt—*blind*—
For sight might magnify some sin,
And make him change his mind!

THE BRADBURY BOYS.

I know how people talk and feel
  About this noise and fuss,
This meeting here to-day between
  The Bradbury boys and us.

How time whirls on—in figuring up
  We find this fact appears:—
Since last we met these Bradbury boys
  'Tis more than fifty years.

Perhaps you know these Bradbury boys—
  If not, you ought to know
This tall, gray fellow here is Cale,
  And then come Ase and Joe.

These other fellows, lubbering round,
  Are all our boys, you see—
Here's Noah and Nat, and Dan and Mark,
  And also Lew and me.

These Bradbury boys—one left his law,
  And one his grapes and corn,
And travelled near a thousand miles
  To find where they were born.

Look :—here's where *old* Joe Bradbury lived—
The place that Bradbury tilled,
And there's the chopping father cleared
The year that he was killed.

And there's where Thomas Townsend dwelt—
Where, on his leathern seat,
He took those measures, year by year
For our tired, pattering feet.

Those feet have trod some slippery paths,
Since death one day so grim,
Took Townsend from his kit of tools,
And then his breath from him.

That broken clam-shell skimmer there,
This moment found by Joe,
His mother used for skimming milk
Some sixty years ago.

Poor Joe—but then my muse can wait
Until your cheeks are dry,
Some think that nought but loss of fees
Can make a lawyer cry.

That wall—hold on—Nat's pigs are out—
  Good gracious what a fuss
Mid pigs and tears to rhyme about
  The Bradbury boys and us.

Don't ask—that thought has bothered me :—
  This *how* and *where* and *when*,
We six shall meet and recognize
  These Bradbury boys again.

Friends of life's early youth accept
  This humble gift of mine,
A wreath wrought with a hurried hand
  Around this pilgrim shrine.

However faint a fickle faith,
  Some future bliss insures,
Amid each agony of doubt
  One present bliss is yours,

If you will bear to western homes
  Old memories fraught with joy,
As Æneas bore Anchises through
  The burning gates of Troy.

THE THIRD CREMATION.

AN INCIDENT OF THE BELFAST FIRE, SEPT., 1873.

Joseph Dennett, sit down with me here on this rock,
Rest your legs and your heart while you list to my talk,
  Keep the smoke from my eyes while I read you my rhyme,
  Take a lunch from my box in exchange for your time;
What! Dennett, see there—why, that looks some to me
Like the cellar and well where your home used to be—
  And the knoll where that burnt, broken bureau is laid,
  Why, it looks like the spot where your children once played.
      Twice before,
      Twice before,
      I have stood at your door,
    When each bell in the spire
    Screamed "*the city's a-fire!*"
  First on that wild night in the years long ago,
  (You remember, I know,)
    When, with borrowed horse dray,
    I bore swiftly away
    The warm couch where you lay—
      When those fire demons came,
      With their tongues all aflame,

And they poured and they swashed their red lava like rain,
And as roof after roof disappeared from the sight,
I remember those fiends—how they rollicked that night!
But your walls, they were brick,
And your walls, they were thick—
So you lined up your charred, gutted castle again;
But now, my tired man,
They have scooped and have cleaned you clear down to the pan.

Joseph Dennett, sit still, and don't hurry one mite,
For I wish to know more of this singular fight—
Of this fight against odds
With the demons or gods.
Say, what have you done and pray what have you said?
Have you wronged the live living, have you wronged the cold dead?
I believe in the warm, fervent prayer of the priest,
And believe in my mother's worn bible, at least;
I believe while we dwell and we grope in the form,
It behooves us to bow now and then to the storm;
But ah, there are times when the blows are too tough—
When the cold, stolid granite is battered enough;
There are times when the act would be cowardly weak,
To incline to the smiter the opposite cheek—
So, old Craftsman, your ear,
And a word on the Square,

If you're *honest*, before I would buckle one hair,
To the Powers in the skies, or the regions below,
I would stand up alone in your desolate woe—
And would say to those powers who have scooped you so clean,
What in heaven do you want—tell me square what you mean;
Must you go? but a word to the close of my rhyme,
Take the rest of my lunch and this scrip for your time.

LAYING OF THE CORNER STONE,

TRINITY CHURCH, EXETER.

Let your mitred Bishop stand
By this upturned yielding sod,
And with consecrated hand
Lay your corner stone to God.

Then with skillful builders' care
Rear aloft your sacred dome,
Raise your steeple high in air
Pointing to a spirit home.

Let no bitter burning brawls
Foully nursed by blended zeal
Ever echo round your walls—
Fatal as the cannon's peal.

To your robed and tutored Priest—
  Acting here his Rector's part—
Let me hold some thoughts at least,
  Gushing warmly from my heart.

Whether pleasure come or pain,
  Whether worldly gain or loss,
When the crucible you drain,
  Give us gold, refined from dross.

With a scholar's loyal lore,
  And a heart imbued with love,
Ever guard your chapel door,
  As they guard the gates above.

Though your armor bids you face
  All the elements of strife,
It will elevate your race
  To a higher plain of life.

Preach the everlasting word
  Free from innovated taints—
Preach the Christ that Peter heard
  As he journeyed with the Saints.

By the help of Him who died
  Aided by redemption's plan,
Bridge the chasm deep and wide
  That has yawned 'twixt God and man.

AN HOUR WITH TOM PLUMADORE.

What, never saw Tom Plumadore—
  Him from the Frenchman nation—
Who runs the tank at Clinton Gore,
  At the old Burnham station?

You know Judge Rice, who sleeps on down—
  Our learned, legal brother—
Him of the *highest* type of man,
  Tom Plumadore the other.

Rice is the famed Maine Central boss—
  Runs that machine of "*hisen;*"
Tom runs the tank—a kind of cross
  'Twixt hell and Libby prison.

For years, within that tank, 'tis said,
  That Bull-Run scarred old fellow,
Has slept, with pea-straw for his bed,
  And beech-log for his pillow.

Oh, strange extremes that meet our eyes,
Which ever way we turn 'em—
Soft down for the sleek limbs of Rice,
And straw for Tom at Burnham!

I tried Tom's bed, and thought, perhaps
My poor, scarred Bull-Run brother
May find some sweeter, pea-straw naps,
Than down may yield the other.

THE ATHEIST'S "LAST LOOK."

The Atheist's child in its coffin slept,
In the village chapel's nook,
Ere the time when the stricken father said,
"'Tis the last look!"

He never heeded the soothing balm,
Which dropped from the holy book,
But only thought of the time he must say,
"'Tis the last look!"

The lid of the coffin was slowly raised,
When the crimson his face forsook,
For he knew that the words must quickly come,
"'Tis the last look!"

He tottered along to the coffin's side,
And his child's cold hand he took,
And uttered a shriek which pierced the heart,
"'Tis the last look!"

And I saw a tear in that Athiest's eye,
And I saw that a Deist shook,
As he uttered those thrilling words once more,
"'Tis the last look!"

Methought if he hoped as a Christian hoped,
And walked by the light of God's book,
He never would murmur those words again,
"'Tis the last look!"

WHAT IS TRUE POETRY.

How many squander off their hours
In rhyming *flea* with *tea*,
And fondly dream it constitutes
The soul of Poetry!

It is not Poetry to frame
A line that ends with *chink*,
And stretch another at its side
That ends with *bobolink*.

It is not Poetry to hook
    A sole idea up,
And spread it (as you spread a salve)
    Around a butter-cup.

The finding but a lonesome thought
    Within a volume, makes
One think of bobbing for an eel,
    Mixed with a pond of snakes.

True Poetry can have no length
    Nor breadth—it never lends
Its body to be measured off
    Upon your fingers' ends.

True Poetry is never decked—
    It always lives undressed—
But has a fire to warm itself,
    Concealed within its breast.

Its joy is this: to find the key
    And keep it in control,
Which fits the lock that closes up
    The chambers of the soul.

And then it labors long and well
To learn the magic art
Of throwing on a screen the lights
And shadows of the heart.

LIGHT.

Brothers, are you faint and weary,
Is your pathway dark and dreary;
Doubt, nor fear, nor falter never,
Let this be your watchword, ever,
Light!

Better days may soon be dawning,
Darkest hours give birth to morning;
Yield not to the fiend Despair,
Keep in mind old Ajax's prayer—
"Light!"

Ask no garb from Nemean lion,
But with heart, and nerves of iron,
Fight your fight in fearless manner,
With this motto on your banner—
Light!

Light to stamp each sin with terror,
Light to hunt and banish error,
Light to kill or weaken sorrow,
Light to gild a better morrow—
Light!

Light to make oppression falter,
Light from truth's own burning altar,
Light to shine on hearts benighted,
Light to see each wrong is righted—
Light!

While one intellect is clowded,
While one soul in sin is shrouded,
While a world for light is dying,
Brother, never cease your crying—
Light!

A THOUGHT.

I wouldn't surrender the exquisite pleasure
  Of soothing a sorrow and drying a tear,
By heaping around me, regardless of measure,
The purest of gold and the choicest of treasure
  Which Dives, while living, inherited here.

I wouldn't add pain to a chord that is aching,
  Nor furrow new lines on the forehead of care,
Nor prove instrumental, ah never, in making
One throb of a poor brother's heart that is breaking,
  Or bleeding from wounds by the blade of despair.

I wouldn't kneel down to the goddess of fashion,
  And list to the notes of her treacherous song,
Nor govern my pulse by the fever of passion,
Nor blindly and madly and recklessly dash on,
  Neglectful of right to the bosom of wrong.

I wouldn't give much to the world that we live in,
  Where fruitful is hatred and barren is love,
Where friendship's foundation is ever upheaving,
And half of existence is squandered in grieving,
  Except for the hopes of a heaven above.

STEAMBOAT KNITTING.

On the 24th day of August, A. D., 1853, an aged widow, fully clad in mourning, sat quietly and busily engaged in knitting a stocking in the saloon of the Steamer *Penobscot*, on her passage from Belfast to Bangor. I observed, to my astonishment, two young women, gorgeously decked, pointing and laughing at the old lady with her knitting work. One of the maidens referred to had a large hole in the heel of her stocking. The foregoing incident suggested the following lines:—

Knit on—let "moderns" giggle if they will,—
Knit on, nor squander thine allotted time;
Knit on, old matron, and my poet's quill
Shall tell thy virtues in these measured rhymes.
Despite of idiot laugh and pointless joke,
I love to see thee at thy knitting-work.

Thou 'mind'st me of those stormy days, old Dame,
When toil like thine was honored more than now,
When, stockingless, through blood and frost and flame,
Our fathers won fresh laurels for the brow;
When "Mother Bailey" raised her warring notes,
And furnished wadding from her petticoats.

When girls were made to "draw" with handle mop
In "water colors," o'er unfinished room,
And taught, on washing-day, the "waltzing hop,"
And learned their "music" at the wheel and loom;
When silk or satin, or the flaunting gauze,
Was bad to milk in when the cows were cross.

When man of brain could triumph o'er his birth,
  When all but monkeys shaved their upper lips,
When *error* met by truth was *"crushed to earth,"*
  When lodge-room was the only place for "grips,"
When boys had *fathers* (now they have a "Pa,")
And lived a space 'twixt nursing and cigar.

I hate to see the meanest reptile die,
  I hate a fop—I hate a mincing prude;
I hate the fret of saw-dust in my eye;
  I hate a thief—I hate ingratitude,
But from mine inmost soul far worse than all
I hate a sneering o'er the sweat of toil,
And worse than sin I hate the wretch that leads
The van to taunt a widow in her weeds;
I loathe the wretch—if for no reason other
I have myself, a stricken, widowed mother.

THE TWO PRISONERS.

I've somewhere read, or heard, or dreamed,
  And which I cannot say,
Of a strange custom, practised long
  By the famed Seneca.

Whene'er a tender maiden dies,
  A mourner quickly brings
A captured bird to keep encaged
  Till some sweet song he sings.

When the chained bird, with dulcet tone,
  Borne by some warrior brave,
Is loosed with many a fond caress
  Above the maiden's grave.

And charged with many a message there,
  From the rude savage band,
To bear on swiftest wing to her
  In the bright spirit land.

Perchance my chafing, struggling soul,
  Imprisoned close and long,
Is kept within these earthly walls
  To test its power of song.

And soon, like the caged Indian bird,
  Let loose, will carry o'er,
Some message to the loved who dwell
  Upon God's shining shore.

AT THE FRONT.

'Tis the usage of years in all wars of the tent—
With the cannon and grape, with the sword and the gun,
That the wounded and weak to the rear shall be sent—
Shall be sent in platoons or be sent one by one—
While the front is made up of the brave and the strong,
Though the battle be short or the battle be long.
But the war I am in—in this war with disease—
With a fear and a tremor the enemy sees,
To this custom of ages they pay no regard,
And I say to my race and to God, it is hard—
It is hard that they send us pale, weak ones ahead,
Thro' the fight and the march that leads down to the dead.

CORNELE.*

I am sick, and have left all my papers and laws,
And am stopping awhile at this tavern of Shaw's;
And I take what a prince or a monarch might get—
Just the best of a meal and an ars'nic pellet—
And this fact should come in: I was here, you should know,
When they opened this house, thirty-nine years ago.
From the crowd that was here in that year '35,
Not a soul do I find 'round this mansion alive,

* Cornelius Crowley, for 39 years head porter at the Bangor House, and who died in 1875.

Not a man—not a one do I find here about,
But the porter, "Cornele," and a Judge with the gout.
Famed "Cornele" with his brush, for the boot or the blouse,
All the world has regarded a part of the house.
What a load he has lugged the world's baggage among!
For the garrulous old and the jubilant young;
And he boasts with a true Celtic pride of the touch,
He has put on the boots of a Webster and such;
And to-day, 'mid his books, right in earnest, not sport,
I have talked on one point, with a Judge of our court—
And he says that in spite of old statutes or creeds
This "Cornele" should now pass by all subsequent deeds.
When his last load is borne, and the famed porter dies,
I would carve on the slab at the spot where he lies:
Here he sleeps, pardoned out from the last of his sin,
Ever true to the faith of his priest and his kin.
Had he faults?—let the world gossip round as it can—
He has blacked and has brushed, and has lugged like a man.
How the dream chills my heart, how the thought makes me feel,
That a breath may blow out the warm lamp of "Cornele"—
Leaving two, only two from that big, ancient crowd,
And those two peering 'round for the turf and the shroud;
One a pale, haggard bard—tottering out on his cane—
And the other the Judge, on his hammock of pain.

KATAHDIN IRON WORKS.

To my couch in Number 6,
Where one Wilder Taylor dwelleth,
Where the good dames round me fix
Those rare trout which Wilder selleth,

Through the darksome, livelong night,
Through the hours to sleep or ponder,
Comes a stream of molten light,
From the Davis foundry yonder.

As the yielding nuggets melt
For the crimson pigs of iron,
How it lights the famous belt
Of the classical Orion

Lights the north star, pinioned there,
Where each race and age have found it,
Lights the blinking Major Bear
In its index tramps around it.

Here the invalid seeks rest—
Seeks the softened nerve to harden,
Sucking from each brawny breast
Iron milk from out Katahdin.

Let the bloated millionaire
  And the worn, demented fogy,
Gloat around some bill of fare,
  Mid the plates of Saratoga,

Let the modern-schooled divine,
  With his faithless creed and flurry,
Shun this cool retreat of mine
  For the Adirondack Murray.

Let some poet—made not born—
  With strange airs, and verse, and metre,
Wake his harp each night and morn,
  Round the relics of St. Peter.

Better come to Number 6,
  Where one Wilder Taylor dwelleth,
Where the good dames round you fix
  Those rare trout which Wilder selleth.

Here the invalid finds rest,
  Finds the softened nerve to harden,
Sucking from each brawny breast
  Iron milk from out Katahdin.

THE UNFINISHED TASK.

I have stood by the unmarked lowly tomb
Of the blacksmith, Hiram Staples,
  Who was made a corse
  When shoeing a horse—
    The old man—Vulcan Staples.
  I have stood mid the gloom
  Of a Virgil's tomb
    In the famous land of Naples,
  And the dirt was the same
  That covered the frame
    Of the old man—Hiram Staples,
  As the dirt that I found
  On the poet's mound
    In the classic land of Naples.
  One went neath the sod
  Ere the horse was shod
    To the home of the Virgin Mary,
  And the other went there,
  Mid his dreams so rare,
    On his visit to Megara.

I was sorry that either went under the sod
Ere the rhymes were finished or the horse was shod,
But we all pass off with a task undone,
Sudden and silent, and one by one,
        Like the old man, Hiram Staples,
    Or the bard who died.
    Mid his fame and pride,
        In the beauteous land of Naples.
But the jobs that we leave unfinished here
We will finish all up in another sphere.

www.ingramcontent.com/pod-product-compliance
Lightning Source LLC
LaVergne TN
LVHW010251110826
845151LV00004B/1439

* 9 7 8 1 4 2 5 5 2 2 9 6 4 *